POCKET
TOPICAL
BIBLE

POCKET TOPICAL BIBLE

A quick subject index to the key Bible verses on over 900 themes, places and persons of the Bible in any translation or version.

PRL2 Pocket Reference Library Edition
ISBN 0-529-07047-2

Cover design by David Versluis Design
Book design by Blue Water Ink

A Meridian Publication
Published with World Bible Publishers

Manufactured in the United States of America

HOW TO USE YOUR TOPICAL BIBLE

"All scripture
is inspired by God
and profitable for teaching . . .
and for training in righteousness,
that the man of God may be complete,
equipped for every good work."
(2 Timothy 3:16–17).

Have you ever wondered what the Bible has to say about certain topics like work, friendship, or marriage? Or have you wondered who Jehu was, or what happened at Jericho? This concise index of the themes, places, and persons of the Bible can help you find the answers. It can give you a quick reference, like where to find the Sermon on the Mount, or it can lead you into an exciting exploration of a theme like forgiveness or evangelism. It can be used with any translation or paraphrase of the Bible.

Of course, using this book is only a beginning. If you want to do further study on a topic, you will need to consult a Bible dictionary, a concordance, or a Bible commentary.

One word of caution: a verse should always be studied in its biblical context; isolating a verse may distort the intended meaning of the Bible passage. Also, for a more complete grasp of a topic, be sure to read each related entry given in parentheses after the primary topical entry; for example: **CONTENTMENT** *(See also Anxiety, Peace)*.

The *Pocket Topical Bible* will guide you into the exciting truths of the Bible. It will help you locate the answers to your questions and will make you feel more at home with God and his Word.

A

AARON (See also Priest, Priesthood)
Family of	Exod 6:16–20; 1 Chron 6:3–15, 50–53
Spokesman for Moses	Exod 4:14–5:21; 7:1–2
Consecrated priest with sons	Exod 28:1–29:46
Fashions golden calf	Exod 32:1–6, 21–25
Jealous of Moses yet repentant	Num 12:1–12
Symbol of priesthood	Ps 115:10, 12

ABANDONMENT (See also Desertion)
Of this world for Christ	Phil 3:7–10
Of men by God because of:	
Rejection of God	Rom 1:21–32
Sin	Heb 10:26–31

ABEDNEGO (See also Meshach, Shadrach)
Youth captured by Nebuchadnezzar	Dan 1:1–7
Saved in fiery furnace	Dan 3:1–30

ABEL (See also Cain)
Account of his life and death	Gen 4:1–8, 25
The first victim of human sin	Matt 23:35
Example of faith	Heb 11:4
Compared with Christ	Heb 12:24

ABIGAIL
Wife of Nabal	1 Sam 25:1–38
Wife of David	1 Sam 25:39–42

ABIHU
Son of Aaron   *Lev. 10:1*
Killed after offering unholy incense   *Lev. 10:2*

ABIJAH
King of Judah   *1 Kings 15:3*
Made war against Israel   *2 Chron 13:1–20*

ABISHAI
Helps David spy on Saul   *1 Sam 26:5–12*
One of David's mighty men   *2 Sam 23:18–19*

ABNER
Commander of Saul's army   *1 Sam 14:50*
Fights against David   *2 Sam 2:8–32*
Aligns with David   *2 Sam 3:8–21*
Murdered by Joab   *2 Sam 3:27*

ABOMINATION *(See also Evil, Sin)*
Idolatry   *Deut 7:25–26*
Sexual immorality   *Lev 18:1–30*
Dishonest trade   *Deut 25:13–16*
Sorcery   *Deut 18:9–13*
Lies   *Prov 12:22*
False worship   *Isa 1:10–15*

ABOMINATION OF DESOLATION
Prophecy of   *Dan 8:11–14; 9:27; 12:11*
Mentioned by Christ   *Matt 24:15; Mark 13:14*

ABORTION

Soul of fetus is implied	*Ps 51:5; 139:13–16*
Penalty for killing fetus	*Exod 21:22–25*

ABRAHAM *(See also Covenant, Sarah)*

His history and God's call	*Gen 11:27–12:7*
Involvement with Lot	*Gen 13:1–14:16; 18:16–33*
Encounter with Melchizedek	*Gen 14:17–24*
Covenant established with God	*Gen 15:1–21*
Fathered Ishmael by Hagar	*Gen 16:1–16; 21:8–21*
Circumcision covenant introduced	*Gen 17:1–14*
Promise of a true son	*Gen 15:4; 18:9–15*
Fulfillment of the promise	*Gen 21:1–7*

ABSALOM

David's son	*2 Sam 3:3*
Conspired against David	*2 Sam 15:1–12*
David fled from	*2 Sam 15:13–17*
Killed by Joab	*2 Sam 18:9–17*
Mourned by David	*2 Sam 18:33*

ABSTINENCE FROM ALCOHOL *(See also Drinking, Drunkenness, Wine)*

By Israel's priests	*Lev 10:8–11*
By Nazirites	*Num 6:3–4*
Wisdom of	*Prov 23:20–21, 29–35*
For a weaker brother's sake	*Rom 14:13–21*
By deacons and elders	*1 Tim 3:2–3, 8; Titus 1:7*

ABUNDANCE *(See also Blessing, Money, Riches)*

God's blessing on the obedient	*Deut 30:9–10*
Subject to God's judgment	*Luke 12:13–21*

Characteristic of:

God's character	*Exod 34:6–7*
God's grace	*Rom 5:17, 20; 1 Tim 1:14*
Christian life	*John 10:10*

ACCUSATION, FALSE *(See also Lying, Persecution)*

Condemned by God	*Exod 20:16; 23:1, 7; Lev 19:16*
Characteristic of Satan	*Rev 12:9–10*

ACHAN

Caused Israelites' rout at Ai	*Josh 7:1–23*
Stoned	*Josh 7:24–26*

ACHISH

King of Gath	*1 Sam 21:10*
David feigns insanity in front of	*1 Sam 21:1–15*

ACTING WISELY *(See also Behavior, Prudence, Wisdom)*

Example of David	*1 Sam 18:5, 14–15, 30*
Part of godly character	*Ps 101:2*

ADAM *(See also Eve, Fall of Man)*

The first man	*Gen 1:26–2:8*
His sin and punishment	*Gen 2:8–3:24*
His role and Christ's compared	*Rom 5:12–21*

ADMONISHMENT *(See also Chastisement, Counsel)*
Duty of:

Fathers	Eph 6:4
Spiritual leaders	1 Thess 5:12
All Christians	Rom 15:14

Sources of:

Scripture	1 Cor 10:11
Wise men	Eccles 12:11–12
Spiritual knowledge	Col 3:16

ADOLESCENCE *(See also Youth)*

Ridicule in	Job 30:1
Mockery in	Prov 30:17
Cursing in	Prov 20:20
Running away from lusts in	2 Tim 2:22
Rejoicing in	Eccles 11:9
Remembering the Creator in	Eccles 12:1
Not to be despised	1 Tim 4:12

Instruction for:

A wise son	Prov 13:1
All youth	Prov 23:22

ADONIJAH

Fourth son of David	1 Kings 1:5, 11, 25
Pardoned by Solomon	1 Kings 1:53

ADOPTION *(See also Family, Fatherhood, Orphan)*

Israel adopted by God	Deut 14:1–2
Gentiles adopted by God	Eph 3:1–6
Through the Spirit	Rom 8:14–17, 23

11

Predestined   *Rom 8:29–30*
Through belief in Christ   *John 1:12–13*
Object of Christ's mission   *Gal 4:4–5*

ADULTERY *(See also Fornication, Lust)*
Forbidden by God   *Exod 20:14; Deut 5:18*
Defined by Christ   *Matt 5:27–28, 32*
Deserves God's judgment   *Heb 13:4*
Symbolic of Israel's sin   *Ezek 16:1–63; Hos 1:2*
Symbolic of worldliness   *James 4:1–5; Rev 17:1–6*

ADVERSITY *(See also Affliction, Pain, Trouble)*
Caused by:
Man's sin   *Gen 3:16–17; Lev 26:14–39*
God's discipline   *Heb 12:5–11*
In order to:
Punish for sin   *1 Sam 12:9–12*
Teach dependence upon God   *Deut 8:2–6*
Purify our faith   *2 Pet 1:5–8*
Produce strong character   *James 1:2–3*

AENEAS
Healing of   *Acts 9:33*

AFFECTION *(See also Friendship, Love)*
Christ claims first place   *Matt 10:37*
Paul modeling Christ's   *Phil 1:8*
To be shown by:
Spouses to each other   *Eph 5:21–33; Titus 2:4*
All Christians to one another   *Rom 12:10*

AFFLICTION *(See also Adversity, Pain, Suffering)*

Of the righteous	*Amos 5:12; Heb 11:35–38*
To teach obedience	*Ps 119:67; Job 5:6–7, 17–18*
To test faith	*Mark 4:17*
Cannot separate believer from God	*Rom 8:35–39*
To be ended by Christ	*1 Thess 1:4–7*

AGABUS

Foretold famine and suffering	*Acts 11:28; 21:10*

AGRICULTURE *(See also Farming, Vine)*

Established by God's direction	*Gen 2:15*
Related to the rhythm of creation	*Gen 8:22*
Image of God's Word	*Isa 55:10–11*
Parables related to	*Matt 13:1–43*
God's providence in	*Matt 5:45; 2 Cor 9:10–12*

AGRIPPA

Paul's defense before	*Acts 25:22–26:32*

AHASUERUS, XERXES *(See also Esther, Haman, Mordecai)*

Made Esther queen	*Esther 1:1; 2:17*
His decree to destroy Jews	*Esther 3:12*
Hanged Haman	*Esther 7:9; 8:7*
Advanced Mordecai	*Esther 9:4*

AHAZIAH

Wicked reign as king of Judah	*2 Kings 8:25*
As king of Israel	*1 Kings 22:40, 49*

Injury, idolatry, judgment, and death   *2 Kings 1:1–17*

AHIMELECH
Helped David   *1 Sam 21:1–6*

AHITHOPHEL
His counsel esteemed   *2 Sam 16:23*
His advice to Absalom   *2 Sam 17:1–4*
His suicide   *2 Sam 17:23*

ALLEGORY *(See also Symbol)*
Of Israel's unfaithfulness   *Ezek 16:1–17:24*
Of Christ as shepherd   *John 10:1–29*
Of the Old and New Covenants   *Gal 4:21–31*
Of Israel and the Gentiles   *Rom 11:13–24*
Of the Christian's armor   *Eph 6:10–18*

ALLIANCE *(See also Diplomacy, Politics)*
Forbidden with idolaters   *Exod 23:32–33; 34:11–16*
Forbidden with unbelievers   *2 Kings 23:31–25:21*
Example of disobedience and punishment   *2 Cor 6:14*

ALTAR *(See also Offering, Sacrifice)*
Earliest example   *Gen 8:20*
Of incense   *Exod 27:1–8; 30:1–10*
Jordan memorial   *Deut 27:1–8*
Of Jeroboam at Bethel   *1 Kings 12:32–33*
Of Ezekiel's vision (burnt offering)   *Ezek 43:13–27*
Of John's vision (incense)   *Rev 8:3–4*

ALTRUISM *(See also Kindness, Love, Selfishness)*
Manifested in:

Service	*Matt 20:26–28*
Seeking another's welfare	*Phil 2:3–4*
Helping the weak	*Acts 20:35; Rom 15:1–3*

Examples:

Moses	*Exod 32:30–34*
Jesus	*John 13:1–20; Phil 2:5–8*
Paul	*1 Cor 9:19–23*

AMASA

Absalom's captain	*2 Sam 17:25*

AMAZIAH

Godly reign as king of Judah	*2 Kings 14:1*
Defeated by Joash, king of Israel	*2 Chron 25:21*

AMBASSADOR *(See also Alliance, Diplomacy, Politics)*
Representative to:

Obtain favor	*Num 20:14–21; 2 Kings 16:7*
Settle disputes	*Judg 11:12–28*
Issue an ultimatum	*2 Kings 19:9–14*
Ask God's blessing	*Jer 37:3*

Symbolic of:

Christ's servants	*2 Cor 5:20*
Paul in particular	*Eph 6:20*

AMBITION *(See also Presumption, Pride, Self-will)*

Evil, example of Babel	*Gen 11:1–9*

Evil, inspired by:

Satan	*Gen 3:1–6; Luke 4:5–8*
Pride	*Isa 14:12–15; 1 Tim 3:6*
Jealousy	*Num 12:1–2*

Godly:

For the best gifts	*1 Cor 12:31*
For holiness	*Phil 3:12–14*
For the spread of the gospel	*Rom 15:20*

AMEN

Used in Old Testament to:

Express agreement	*Num 5:22*
Affirm a doxology	*1 Chron 16:36*
Confirm an oath	*Neh 5:13*

In the New Testament:

Emphatic closing to benedictions	*Rom 15:33; 16:25–27*
Emphasized the truth of a statement	*John 3:3, 5, 11*
Uttered through Christ	*2 Cor 1:20*

AMMON

Children of	*Gen 19:38*
Prophecies concerning nation	*Jer 25:21*

AMNON

Son of David	*2 Sam 3:2*
Raped half-sister Tamar	*2 Sam 13:1–22*

AMOS

Shepherd called to prophesy	*Amos 1:1; 7:14*
Told by priest not to prophesy	*Amos 7:16*

Saw vision depicting Israel's end   *Amos 8:1–2*

AMUSEMENT *(See also Games, Pleasure)*

The futility of   *Eccles 7:2–6*
Example of Moses' renunciation of   *Heb 11:25*
May lead to rejection of God   *Job 21:12–16*
May lead to spiritual death   *Luke 8:14; 1 Tim 5:6*
Pursuing this indicates sinfulness   *1 Pet 4:3–5*
Part of the rejection of God's prophets   *Rev 11:10*

ANANIAS

(and Sapphira) Their lie and death   *Acts 5:1*
The disciple, sent to Paul   *Acts 9:10*
The high priest, Paul brought before   *Acts 22:30*

ANARCHY *(See also Government, Society)*
Typical of:
Israel before the kingdom   *Judg 17:6; 18:1–31*
The condition of Israel under judgment   *Isa 3:5–8*
The day of antichrist   *2 Thess 2:3–12*
Demonstrated by:
Rampant immorality   *Exod 32:1–8, 25*
Unchecked injustice and violence   *Hab 1:1–4*
Spiritual confusion and idolatry   *Judg 17:1–13*

ANCESTORS *(See also Family, Genealogy)*
God's faithfulness to them   *Lev 26:45*
Character perpetuated in descendants   *Jer 11:10*

ANCHOR, SPIRITUAL *(See also Hope)*

Of the soul   *Heb 6:19*

ANCIENT OF DAYS *(See also God)*

Title applied to God the Father   *Dan 7:9, 13, 22*

ANDREW

One of the apostles   *Matt 10:2; Acts 1:13*

ANGELS *(See also Cherubim, Gabriel, Michael, Seraphim)*

Spiritual servants of God   *Heb 1:14*
Heralds of Christ   *Matt 1:20–21; 28:5–7;*
                                            Luke 2:10–12; Acts 1:9–11

Ministry to believers:
Guidance   *Gen 24:7, 40; Acts 8:26*
Provision for needs   *1 Kings 19:5–8*
Protection and deliverance   *Ps 34:7*
Comfort   *Acts 27:23–24*

Ministry to unbelievers:
Destruction   *Gen 19:13*
Cursing   *Judg 5:23*
Sudden death   *Acts 12:23*
Execution of judgment   *Matt 13:41–42, 49–50*

ANGER *(See also Hatred, Wrath)*

Evil   *Gen 4:6; 49:7; Ps 37:8; Prov 22:24; Matt 5:22*
God's, over sin   *Num 32:10–15*
Christ's   *Mark 3:5*
Must be dealt with   *Eph 4:26–27*

ANIMALS *(See also Birds, Offering, Sacrifice)*

Clean and unclean   *Lev 11:1–31; Acts 10:9–15*
For sacrifices   *Lev 5:6–10; 16:3–5; Exod 12:3–6*
Symbolic of world empires   *Dan 7:2–8*

ANNA

Prophetess who finally saw Messiah   *Luke 2:36*

ANNAS

High priest who judges Christ   *John 18:13, 24*
Peter and John brought before him   *Acts 4:6*

ANOINTED ONE *(See also Messiah)*

Foreshadowed in the Old Testament   *Isa 61:1*
Confirmed in Christ   *Matt 16:16, 20; Luke 4:18–19;*
                                    Acts 4:26–27; 9:22; Heb 1:9

ANOINTING *(See also Dedication, Oil)*

Symbolizes sanctification   *Exod 30:22–32*
Physical, performed upon:
Priests   *Exod 29:7*
Prophets   *1 Kings 19:16*
Kings   *1 Sam 10:1; 1 Kings 19:15–16*
Spiritual, by the Holy Spirit:
Predicted by Joel   *Joel 2:28–29*
Predicted by Christ   *John 7:38–39*
Received at Pentecost   *Acts 2:1–4*
Received at conversion   *John 2:20, 27; 1 Cor 12:13*

ANTHROPOMORPHISM

Physical examples:

Feet and hands	*Exod 24:10–11*
Mouth	*Num 12:8*
Eyes	*Hab 1:13; 1 Pet 3:12*

Non-physical examples:

Change of mind	*Gen 6:6; Exod 32:14*
Consideration of a matter	*Gen 18:17–21*
Memory	*Gen 9:6; Exod 2:24*

ANTICHRIST

Coming predicted	*2 Thess 2:3–12: 1 John 2:18; Rev 11:7*
Characteristic attitude: denying God	*2 Thess 2:3–4*
Deceiver of the world	*2 John 7; Rev 19:20*
Persecutor of Christians	*Rev 13:7*
Epitome of general sin	*2 Thess 2:3, 7*
To be destroyed at Christ's return	*2 Thess 2:8; Rev 19:20*

ANXIETY *(See also Care, Stress, Worry)*

Characteristic of a godless life	*Matt 6:31–32*

Overcome by:

Putting God's will first	*Matt 6:33*
A realistic perspective on life	*Matt 6:34*
Trust in the Lord	*Ps 37:1–7*
Reliance upon the Holy Spirit	*Mark 13:11*
Confidence in God	*Rom 8:28–39*
Commitment to God	*Phil 4:6–7; 1 Pet 5:6–7*

APOLLOS

Eloquent in the Scriptures	*Acts 18:24; 19:1*

APOSTASY *(See also Backsliding, Heresy, Idolatry)*

Of an individual	*1 Sam 15:11; Heb 3:12*
Of a nation	*1 Kings 12:25–33*
Of angels	*2 Pet 2:4; Rev 12:7–9*
Punishment is certain	*Heb 10:26–29*

Caused by:

Evil influences	*Matt 13:20–21; Acts 20:29–30*
Evil desires	*2 Tim 4:3–4*
Spiritual disease	*Acts 28:25–27*

APOSTLE *(See also Disciple, Witness)*

Title of Jesus	*Heb 3:1*
Designation of the Twelve	*Luke 6:13–16*
Listing of the Twelve	*Matt 10:2–4*

Appointed to:

Preach the gospel	*Matt 28:19–20; Acts 1:8*
Write Scripture	*Eph 3:4–5*
Establish the church	*Eph 2:20*

APPAREL *(See also Clothing)*

Symbolizes:

God's judgment	*Isa 63:1–3*
God's selection of his people	*Ezek 16:8–14*
God's redemption	*Zech 3:1–7*
The church's purity	*Rev 19:7–8*

APPEARANCE

Of Christ:

On the cross	*Isa 52:14; 53:7*
At the transfiguration	*Matt 17:2*

21

At the grave of Lazarus   *John 11:38*
Of his hands and side   *John 20:20, 27*

AQUILA
Husband of Priscilla   *Acts 18:2*
Tentmaker driven out of Rome   *Acts 18:2*
Went with Paul to Ephesus   *Acts 18:19*
Commended   *Rom 16:3; 1 Cor 16:19*

ARGUMENT *(See also Quarrel, Strife)*
Forbidden in secondary matters   *Rom 14:1*
Used by Paul in his evangelism   *Acts 9:29; 17:17; 19:8–9*
Characteristic of evil men   *1 Tim 6:4–5*
Example of Job's   *Job 23:1–7*

ARK *(See also Ark of the Covenant)*
Noah's   *Gen 6:5–8:19; 1 Pet 3:20–21*

ARK OF THE COVENANT *(See also Tabernacle)*
Description   *Exod 25:10–22*
Expression of God's holines   *Lev 16:2–3;*
                              1 Sam 6:19–20; 2 Sam 6:6–7
Place of atonement   *Lev 16:2, 13–17; Heb 9:1–10*
Type of Christ   *Heb 9:11–14*

ARM OF GOD *(See also Anthropomorphism)*
As a symbol of God's power in:
Creation   *Jer 27:5; 32:17*
The Exodus   *Exod 6:6; 15:16; Deut 11:2*
Preserving his people   *Deut 33:27*

| Judgment | *Ps 89:10, 13; Jer 21:5* |
| Redemption | *Isa 40:10–11* |

ARMAGEDDON
| Site of end-time battle | *Rev 16:16* |

ARMOR *(See also War, Weapon)*
| Goliath's and Saul's | *1 Sam 17:5–7, 38–39* |

As symbol:
| Of Christian character | *Rom 13:12* |
| Of spiritual resources | *Eph 6:11–17* |

ARMY *(See also War)*
Israel's first	*Josh 5:13–6:5*
Symbolic of the church	*Eph 6:12; 2 Cor 10:3–6*
End-time armies	*Dan 11:7–45; 19:19*

ARREST
Of Jesus in Gethsemane	*Matt 26:50: Mark 14:46*
Of apostles after Pentecost	*Acts 5:17–18; 6:12*
Of Paul and Silas	*Acts 16:19*
Of Paul	*Acts 21:30–33*

ARROGANCE *(See also Boasting, Conceit, Pride)*
Condemned	*1 Sam 2:3*
Hated by God	*Prov 8:13*
To be judged by God	*Isa 13:11*
Crucial sin of Moab	*Jer 48:29*

ART *(See also Creativity)*

Early development	*Gen 4:21–22*
Expression of service to God	*Exod 31:1–11*

ASA

Godly king of Judah	*1 Kings 15:9, 11*
Wrongly sought aid of Syrians	*2 Chron 16:1–10*
Death of	*2 Chron 16:11–14*

ASAHEL

Killed by Abner in self-defense	*2 Sam 2:18–23*

ASCENSION *(See also Resurrection)*

Of Enoch	*Gen 5:24; Heb 11:5*
Of Elijah	*2 Kings 2:11*
Of Jesus Christ	*Mark 16:19; Luke 24:50; Acts 1:9–11*
Beginning of Christ's exaltation	*Acts 2:32–36*

ASCETICISM *(See also Abstinence from alcohol, Celibacy, Fasting)*

Old Testament examples	*Num 6:1–21*
Characteristic of John the Baptist	*Matt 3:4; 11:18*
Rebuked by Paul	*Col 2:20–23; 1 Tim 4:1–5*
Positive teaching	*1 Cor 9:24–27; 2 Tim 2:3–5*

ASHER

Son of Jacob	*Gen 30:13*
Inheritance in Promised Land	*Josh 19:24*

ASHERAH, ASHERIM

Images of Canaanite religion	*Deut 6:5*
Removed by Asa	*2 Chron 14:5*
Removed by Jehoshaphat	*2 Chron 17:6*
Worshiped by Judah	*2 Chron 24:17–18*

ASHES *(See also Mourning, Sorrow)*
Symbolic of:

Purification	*Num 19:17–19; Heb 9:13*
Mourning	*2 Sam 13:19; Esth 4:1, 3; Isa 61:3*
Repentance	*Job 42:6; Matt 11:21*
Humility before God	*Dan 9:3*

ASHTAROTH

Goddess of Canaanites	*Josh 9:10*

Idolatrous worship of:

By Israel	*Judg 2:13; 1 Sam 12:10*
By Solomon	*1 Kings 11:5, 33*

ASSAULT AND BATTERY *(See also Beating)*

Old Testament laws	*Exod 21:15, 18–19*
Jesus' comments	*Matt 5:38–39*
Jesus as victim	*Matt 26:67; 27:30; Mark 14:65*

ASSEMBLY *(See also Church)*
Term for:

Israel as a nation	*Judg 20:2; 2 Chron 30:23*
God's elect people	*Ps 111:1*
A community meeting	*Acts 19:32, 39, 41*
A local church	*James 2:2*

The heavenly church   *Heb 12:23*

ASSURANCE *(See also Confidence, Hope)*
Rooted in faith   *Eph 3:20; 2 Tim 1:12; Heb 10:22*
Expressed in hope   *Heb 6:11, 19*
Confirmed by love   *John 3:14, 18–19; 4:18*
Resting in God's power   *John 10:28–30*
Sealed by Christ's work   *Rom 8:28–39*
Witnessed to by the Spirit   *Rom 8:15–16*

ASTROLOGY *(See also Magic, Star, Witchcraft)*
Vain hope   *Isa 47:12–15*
Vain help   *Dan 5:7–8*
Vanity, compared with God   *Dan 2:27–28*

ASTRONOMY *(See also Star)*
Guide to God's handiwork   *Gen 1:3–8; Job 38:31–33;*
                                          Ps 8:3; 19:1–6; Amos 5:8
Stars as symbol of Israel   *Gen 15:5; Jer 31:35–37; 33:22*

ATHALIAH
Daughter of Ahab, mother of Ahaziah   *2 Kings 8:26*
Killed royal family   *2 Kings 11:1; 2 Chron 22:10*
Killed by order of Jehoiada   *2 Kings 11:16*

ATHEISM *(See also Apostasy)*
Characteristic of the wicked   *Ps 10:4; Rom 1:20–32*
Characteristic of the fool   *Ps 14:1; 53:1*
Example of Pharaoh   *Exod 5:2*

ATONEMENT *(See also Atonement, Day of; Justification; Propitiation)*

Sin offering ritual	*Lev 16:1–34*
Accepted by God for forgiveness	*Lev 5:10–13*
Work of Christ	*Rom 3:22–25; Heb 9:11–14*

ATONEMENT, DAY OF

Time specified	*Lev 16:29–31, 34; 23:27*
Ritual specified	*Lev 16:1–34; 23:26–32*
Type of Christ's sacrifice	*Heb 9:11–14*

ATTRIBUTES OF GOD *(See God)*

AUTHORITY *(See also Ruler, Sovereignty)*

Jesus taught with	*Matt 7:29*
To forgive sin	*Matt 9:6*
To cast out demons	*Mark 3:15*
In heaven and on earth	*Matt 28:18*
None, except from God	*Rom 13:1*
Submit to	*Titus 3:1*

AVARICE *(See also Covetousness, Greed)*

An example of vain desire	*Eccles 4:7–8; 5:10–11*
Not characteristic of a Christian elder	*1 Tim 3:2*
Produces grief	*1 Tim 6:9–10*
Once led to national crisis	*Josh 7:1–26*
Once led to an innocent's death	*1 Kings 21:1–14*

AVENGER OF BLOOD

First description	*Gen 9:5*

Mosaic laws	Num 35:19–29; Deut 19:4–13
Laws restated	Josh 20:1–9
Law set aside by David	2 Sam 14:4–14

AWE *(See also Fear, Reverence)*

| Proper reaction to God | Ps 33:8 |
| Proper reaction to God's Word | Ps 119:161 |

B

BAAL *(See also Idolatry)*

| Pagan male deity | Judg 10:6; 1 Sam 7:4 |

Worship of:

Involved immorality	Num 25:1–5; Hos 9:10
Involved idolatry and atrocities	1 Kings 19:18
Introduced to Israel by Ahab	1 Kings 16:30–32
Elijah's triumph over	1 Kings 18:17–40
Denounced by Jeremiah	Jer 2:8, 23; 7:9

BABEL *(See also Babylon)*

| Story of its famous tower | Gen 11:1–9 |

BABY *(See also Children)*

Declare God's glory	Ps 8:2
Description of new believer	1 Pet 2:2
Symbol of immaturity	1 Cor 3:1–2; Heb 5:13

BABYLON *(See also Babel, Nebuchadnezzar)*

| Mighty, ancient kingdom | Dan 4:30; Isa 13:19; 14:4 |

Conqueror of Jerusalem	2 Chron 36:17–21
Destruction predicted	Isa 13:1–22; Jer 50:1–46
Symbol of evil society	Rev 17:1–18:24

BACKBITING (See also Gossip, Slander)

Not characteristic of godly	Ps 15:1–3; 1 Pet 2:1
Characteristic of evil	Rom 1:18, 30; 2 Cor 12:20
Produces angry response	Prov 25:23
Will be judged	Ps 101:5

BACKSLIDING (See also Apostasy)

Early warnings against	Lev 26:14–42; Deut 4:9; 8:11
Demonstrated in parable	Mark 4:7, 15–19
Christ's warnings	Luke 9:62; John 15:6
Paul recounts Israel's	1 Cor 10:1–13
To be repented of	Rev 2:4–5; 3:2–3

BAD COMPANY (See also Worldliness)

Contagious sin	Num 16:26
Avoided by good men	Ps 1:1; 26:4–5
Compared with God's company	Ps 84:10
To be shunned	Prov 1:10–19; Rom 16:17–18
Partnership with forbidden	2 Cor 6:14–16

BALAAM

| Story of | Num 22:1–24:25; 31:8 |
| Symbol of evil teachers | 2 Pet 2:15; Jude 11; Rev 2:14 |

BANISHMENT

| Adam and Eve from Eden | Gen 3:22–24 |

Cain	Gen 4:12–14
Israel into exile	2 Chron 36:20–21
The Jews from Rome	Acts 18:2
Satan from heaven	Rev 12:7–9
The wicked to hell	Rev 20:15; 21:8

BAPTISM *(See also John the Baptist)*

By John the Baptist	Matt 3:5–12
Jesus' baptism	Matt 3:11, 13–17
Commanded by Christ	Matt 28:19–20
In the early church	Acts 8:12, 36–38; 9:17–18
By the Holy Spirit:	
Predicted by prophets	Joel 2:28–29
Predicted by Christ	Acts 1:5
At Pentecost	Acts 2:16–21

BARABBAS

| Exchanged for Christ before Pilate | Matt 27:16–26 |
| Referred to by Peter | Acts 3:14 |

BARNABAS

Early example of sharing	Acts 4:36–37
Supporter of Paul	Acts 9:27; 11:22–26; 13:1–14:28
Addressed Jerusalem council	Acts 15:1–35
Separation from Paul	Acts 15:36–40
Paul's testimony about	1 Cor 9:6; Gal 2:1, 9, 13

BARRENNESS *(See also Sterility)*

| A reproach | Gen 16:2; 30:22–23 |
| A judgment | 2 Sam 6:23 |

The absence of God's blessing	*Exod 23:26*
Removed by God	*Ps 113:9*
Jesus' response to a fig tree	*Mark 11:12–14, 20–22*
Defense against spiritual	*2 Pet 1:5–8*

BARTHOLOMEW

One of the apostles	*Matt 10:3; Acts 1:13*

BARTIMAEUS

Blind beggar healed by Jesus	*Mark 10:46–52*

BATHING *(See also Washing)*

Of Pharaoh's daughter	*Exod 2:5*
Of Bathsheba	*2 Sam 11:2*
For refreshment of feet	*Gen 24:32; John 13:10*
For ceremonial cleansing	*Lev 14:8; 2 Kings 5:10–14*
As part of Jewish rituals	*Mark 7:2*

BATHSHEBA

Relationship with David	*2 Sam 11:1–27*
Children born to	*2 Sam 12:14–19, 24; 1 Chron 3:5*
Secures throne for Solomon	*1 Kings 1:11–31*
Adonijah's dealings with	*1 Kings 2:13–25*

BATTLE *(See also Army, War)*

Gideon against the Midianites	*Judg 7:20–21*
Involving priests	*2 Chron 13:12*
Prayer preceding it	*2 Chron 14:11; 20:3–12*

31

BEARD *(See also Hair)*

Long, worn by leaders	*Ps 133:2; Judg 16:17*
Sign of holiness	*Lev 19:27; 21:5*

BEATING *(See also Assault and Battery)*

For the disobedient	*Luke 12:47–48*
Unjust, of a servant	*Luke 20:10–11*
Of Christ	*Isa 50:6; Mark 15:19*
Of the apostles	*Acts 5:40*
Of Paul	*Acts 16:19–24*

BEAUTY *(See also Art)*

Vanity of it	*Prov 31:30*
Danger of it	*Prov 6:25–29; 2 Sam 11:2–5*
Symbolized:	
God's care	*Hos 14:6; Matt 6:28–29*
In the Messiah and his bride	*Ps 45:2–3, 8, 11–14*
In Zion	*Ps 50:2*
In the feet of preachers	*Isa 52:7; Rom 10:15*

BEELZEBUB

Prince of devils	*Matt 12:24; Mark 3:22*

BEGGAR *(See also Poverty)*

Not the fate of the righteous	*Ps 37:25*
Cursed state	*Ps 109:8–11*
Christ's contact with	*Mark 10:46–52*
Parable of Lazarus	*Luke 16:19–31*
Peter's and John's healing of	*Acts 3:1–10*

BEHAVIOR *(See also Conduct, Morality)*

Toward neighbor	*Matt 7:12; Rom 15:2*
In accord with Christ	*Rom 15:5*
That glorifies God	*Rom 15:6*
Toward enemies	*Matt 5:39–42*

BELIEF *(See also Confidence, Faith, Unbelief)*

Godly response	*Gen 15:6; John 1:7, 12; 3:16*
Results in victory	*2 Chron 20:20–30; Mark 9:17–27*
Integral to Jesus' preaching	*Mark 1:15; 11:22–24*
Part of early confession	*Rom 10:9*
Mark of the true Christian	*1 John 5:13*

BELIEVER *(See Belief, Christian, Disciple)*

BELSHAZZAR

Writing on the wall	*Dan 5:1–6*
His judgment by Daniel, his death	*Dan 5:13–30*

BENEDICTION

Earliest example	*Gen 1:22, 28*
Pronounced upon Abraham	*Gen 14:19–20*
By Jacob upon his sons	*Gen 48:15–49:28*
Priestly, instituted by God	*Deut 10:8; 21:5*
Aaronic	*Num 6:23–26*
Mosaic	*Deut 33:1–29*
Pronounced upon Jesus	*Luke 2:34–35*
Pronounced by Jesus	*Luke 24:50*
Pronounced by the apostles	*Rom 15:5–6, 13*

BENEFICENCE *(See also Benevolence, Generosity, Liberality, Kindness)*

Ordained by the Law	*Deut 15:7–15, 18*
Blessing upon those who give	*Ps 41:1; Prov 22:9*
Characteristic of God	*Ps 112:9*
Ordained by Christ	*Matt 5:42; 25:35–45; Mark 9:41*
In the early church	*Acts 6:1–6; 2 Cor 8:1–6*
Rewarded in heaven	*1 Tim 6:17–19*
Lack of, cursed	*Prov 28:27; 1 Tim 5:8; 1 John 3:17*

BENEVOLENCE *(See also Charity, Love)*

Toward the poor and needy	*Gal 2:10; Eph 4:28*
Toward enemies	*Prov 25:21–22; Matt 5:39, 43–44*
Useless if not motivated by love	*1 Cor 13:3*
Worth of is relative to giver	*Mark 12:41–44*
Part of Christian responsibility	*Rom 12:13*
A sacrifice pleasing to God	*Heb 13:16*
Brings blessing	*Prov 11:25; Isa 58:10–11; Acts 20:35*

BEN-HADAD

King of Assyria allied with Asa	*1 Kings 15:18*
Baffled by Elisha	*2 Kings 6:8*
Besieged Samaria	*2 Kings 6:24*
Killed by Hazael	*2 Kings 8:7*

BENJAMIN

Individual:

His birth	*Gen 35:16–18*
His visit to Egypt	*Gen 43:1–45:15*

The tribe:

Prophecies about	*Gen 49:27; Deut 33:12*
Scandal, war, and renewal	*Judg 19:1–21:23*
Famous people from	*1 Sam 9:1–2; Phil 3:5*

BEREAVEMENT *(See also Death, Grief, Mourning)*

Examples of accompanying emotions:

Sorrow	*Gen 37:34–35; Exod 12:29–30*
Deep feeling	*2 Sam 18:33*
Bitterness	*Ruth 1:20–21*

Godly responses:

Submission	*Job 1:20–22*
Hope	*John 11:21–27; 1 Thess 4:13–18*
Sorrow	*John 11:35; Acts 9:39*

BETHANY

Location	*Luke 19:29; John 11:18*
Home of Mary, Martha and Lazarus	*John 11:1*
Scene of the Ascension	*Luke 24:50–51*

BETHEL

Jacob dreamed there and named it	*Gen 28:10–19*
Renewal of Jacob's covenant there	*Gen 35:1–15*

BETHLEHEM

Place of Messiah's birth	*Mic 5:2; Matt 2:1, 5*
Where infants were killed	*Jer 31:15; Matt 2:16*

BETRAYAL *(See also Treason)*

Of Samson by Delilah	*Judg 16:15–20*

Of Abner by Joab	*2 Sam 3:26–27*
Guilt of Judas	*Matt 27:3–8*

Of Christ:

Predicted	*Ps 41:9; Matt 17:22*
Betrayer identified	*John 13:21–30*
In Gethsemane	*Matt 26:14–15, 47–50*

BETROTHAL *(See also Marriage)*

Of Jacob	*Gen 29:18–30*
Of Mary and Joseph	*Matt 1:18; Luke 1:27*

Figurative of:

Israel's relationship to God	*Hos 2:19–20*
Church's relationship to Christ	*2 Cor 11:2*

BIGOTRY *(See also Racism, Tolerance)*

Examples of:

Haman toward Jews	*Esther 3:1–11*
Jews toward Samaritans	*John 4:9*
Jews toward Christians	*1 Thess 2:14–16*
Jews toward Gentiles	*Acts 10:28*
Among believers	*Gal 2:11–14*

BILDAD

Friend of Job	*Job 2:11*
His answers to Job	*Job 8; 18; 25*

BIRDS *(See also Animals)*

Created and sustained by God	*Gen 1:20–21*
Sent by divine providence	*Exod 16:12–31*
Used in sacrifices	*Lev 1:14; Luke 2:24*

BIRTH *(See also Baby, Incarnation, Motherhood)*
Of Jesus:
Foretold; fulfilled   Mic 5:2; Matt 1:18
Spiritual:
New   John 3:3–8; 1 Pet 1:23

BIRTHRIGHT *(See also Firstborn, Heir, Inheritance)*
Lost:
By Esau to Jacob   Gen 25:29–34; 27:6–40
By Reuben because of sin   Gen 49:3–4
By Manasseh to Ephraim   Gen 48:15–20

BISHOP *(See also Elder)*
Qualifications   1 Tim 3:1–7; Titus 1:6–9
Duties   Acts 20:17, 28–30
Responsibilities   1 Thess 5:14; Heb 13:17
Exhortation to, by Peter   1 Pet 5:1–3

BITTERNESS *(See also Anger, Retaliation)*
Of water   Exod 15:23–25
Of Passover herbs   Exod 12:8; Num 9:11
A result of sin   Prov 5:4; Acts 8:23
To be avoided:
In personal relationships   Eph 4:31; Col 3:21
As sin   Heb 12:15; James 3:14

BLASPHEMY *(See also Profanity, Swearing)*
Forbidden by God:
The Law   Exod 20:7; Lev 19:12; Deut 5:11
Example of punishment   Lev 24:10–16

Against the Holy Spirit   Matt 12:31–32; Luke 12:10

BLESSEDNESS *(See also Happiness, Joy)*
Condition of those who:

Are forgiven by God	Ps 32:1–2
Are disciplined by god	Ps 94:12
Identify with God	Matt 5:3–12
Are chosen in Christ	Eph 1:3–4
Believe	Gal 3:9
Are justified	Rom 4:5–9

BLESSING *(See also Abundance, Reward)*

Result of obedience	Deut 28:1–2
Comes from God	Prov 3:1–2; James 1:17
Physical	Deut 28:1–14
Of Israelites	Rom 9:4–5
Spiritual	Ps 23; Isa 40:11, 29, 31; Rom 8:1–2, 26–39

BLINDNESS *(See also Darkness)*

Sent by God as judgment	Gen 19:11; Deut 28:28
Healed by Jesus	Matt 9:27–30; 20:30–34
Spiritual	Prov 4:19; Matt 6:23

Spiritual condition of:

Jewish leaders	Matt 15:14; 23:19, 24, 26
Israel	2 Cor 3:14–16
Unbelievers and the disobedient	2 Cor 4:3–4

BLOOD *(See also Atonement, Offering, Sacrifice)*

Symbolizes life	Gen 9:4–6; Lev 17:11, 14; Matt 27:24
Forbidden as food	Gen 9:4; Lev 3:17

Importance in sacrificial system   *Heb 9:22*
Plague upon Egypt   *Exod 7:17–24*
Christ's:
Atonement, propitiation   *Heb 9:12–14, 18–28*
Symbolized in the wine   *Matt 26:28*
Operative today   *1 John 1:7; Rev 12:11*

BOASTING *(See also Arrogance, Conceit, Pride)*

Proper, in God   *Ps 34:2; 2 Cor 10:13–17*
Vain, because of:
The uncertainty of life   *Prov 27:1*
The sovereignty of God   *Luke 12:16–21*
Salvation by grace   *Eph 2:8–9*

BOAZ

Conduct toward Ruth   *Ruth 2–4*
Ancestor of David and Christ   *Matt 1:5; Luke 3:23, 32*

BODY

Made by God   *Gen 2:7, 21–22; Ps 139:13–14*
Subject to death   *Rom 5:12*
Christ's:
Formed by God   *Luke 1:34–35*
Like ours   *Heb 2:14; 4:15*
Resurrected without corruption   *Acts 2:31*
Symbolized in the bread   *Mark 14:22*
Descriptive of the church   *Eph 1:22–23; Col 1:24*

BOLDNESS *(See also Confidence, Courage)*

The result of faith in God   *Prov 14:26; 28:1*

39

| Given through Christ | Eph 3:12; Heb 4:15–16 |

Should be characteristic of:

Fellowship with God	Heb 10:19–22
Preaching	Acts 9:27–29; Eph 6:19; Phil 1:14
Christian hope	1 John 2:28; 4:17

BONDAGE *(See also Captivity, Liberty, Servant)*

Israel in Egypt	Exod 1:7–22; 2:23; 6:6
Israel in Assyria	2 Kings 17:6, 20–23
Judah in Babylon	2 Kings 25:8–12
An individual in Israel	Lev 25:39–43

Figurative of:

Sinful condition	John 8:34; Rom 6:6–17
Submission to the Law	Gal 4:21–5:1
Devotion to Christ	Rom 1:1; 6:18, 22; Phil 1:1

BOOK

| Characteristics of ancient | Jer 36:2; 2 Tim 4:13 |

Of the Law:

Foundation of Israel's religion	Deut 28:58
Lost and found	2 Kings 22:8
Brought renewal	2 Kings 23:2–14, Neh 8:2–3, 8–18

Of Life:

| Contents | Mal 3:16–18; Phil 4:3; Rev 13:8; 17:8 |
| Effects | Luke 10:20; Heb 12:23; Rev 20:12–15 |

BRANCH, SYMBOLIC *(See also Growth, Vine)*

Israel as	Isa 4:2; Rom 11:17–24
Christians and non-Christians as	John 15:2–8
Messiah as	Isa 11:1

BREAD *(See also Communion, Food, Manna)*

Unleavened, for Passover	*Exod 12:15, 17–20*
In the tabernacle	*Lev 24:5–9; Heb 9:2*
Miraculous provision of	*1 Kings 17:6; Matt 14:19–21*
Figurative, of Christ	*John 6:32–35, 48–51*
To commemorate Christ's sacrifice	*Luke 22:7, 19;*
	1 Cor 22:23–29
Sharing of symbolizes fellowship	*Acts 2:42*

BREASTPLATE *(See also Armor)*

For high priest	*Exod 28:15–30*
Worn by soldiers	*1 Sam 17:5*
Symbol of righteousness	*Isa 59:17; Eph 6:14*

BRIBERY

As sin	*Exod 23:8; Ps 26:10; Isa 1:23; Amos 5:12*
Will be punished	*Amos 2:6*
Examples:	
Balak	*Num 22:17, 37*
Delilah	*Judg 16:5*
Soldiers	*Matt 28:11–15*
Unsuccessful by Simon Magus	*Acts 8:18*
Hoped for by Felix	*Acts 24:25–26*

BRIDE *(See also Bridegroom, Marriage, Wife)*

Brings joy to husband	*Isa 62:5*
Symbolizes Israel	*Ezek 16:8–14*
Symbolizes church	*2 Cor 11:2; Eph 5:31–32; Rev 21:2, 9*

BRIDEGROOM *(See also Bride, Husband, Marriage)*

Rejoices over bride	*Isa 62:5*
To separate from former home	*Gen 2:24; Eph 5:31*
Exempted from military duty	*Deut 24:5*
Symbolizes God	*Isa 62:5; Ezek 16:8–14*
Symbolizes Christ	*2 Cor 11:2; Eph 5:31–32; Rev 21:2, 9*

BROTHER *(See also Family)*

First example	*Gen 4:1–2*
A fellow Christian	*Matt 23:8; 1 Cor 8:11; James 2:15*

BURIAL *(See also Death)*

Treatment of body	*Gen 50:26; Matt 26:12; John 11:44*
Rites surrounding	*Gen 23:4–6; Jer 34:5, John 11:19*
Famous:	
Abraham and Sarah	*Gen 23:19; 25:8–10*
David	*1 Kings 2:10*
Jesus	*John 19:38–42*

BURNT OFFERING *(See also Offering, Sacrifice)*

Atonement its purpose	*Lev 1:4*
Laws concerning	*Lev 1:11–17; 6:9–13; 17:8–9*
Offered during special feasts	*Lev 23:26–38*
Offered daily	*Exod 29:38–42; Num 28:1–8*

BUSINESS *(See also Commerce, Finances, Vocation)*

Proper attitudes:	
Desire to put God first	*Matt 6:33; Col 3:17, 23–24*
Warnings about	*Matt 6:19–21; Luke 12:13–21, 34*
Using gifts to the fullest	*Rom 12:8, 11*

Freedom from anxiety	*Matt 6:25–34*
Responsibility to tithe	*Mal 3:8–10*

Good examples:

Joseph	*Gen 41:33–49*
Officers and workmen	*2 Chron 34:8–13*
Daniel	*Dan 6:1–5*
Mordecai	*Esther 10:2–3*

C

CAESAREA

Home of Philip and Cornelius	*Acts 8:40; 10:1*
Home of Herod and Felix	*Acts 18:19–23; 23:23–24*
Peter preached there	*Acts 10:34–43*
Paul preached there	*Acts 9:30*
Paul imprisoned and tried there	*Acts 23:23–26:32*

CAIN *(See also Abel)*

Life, sin, and punishment	*Gen 4:1–17*
Called "of the evil one"	*1 John 3:12*

CALAMITY *(See also Affliction, Suffering)*

Kinds of:

Personal, to Job	*Job 1:13–2:13*
National, to Judah	*Lam 1:1–22*
World-wide	*Matt 24:5–31; Luke 21:25–28*

Because of:

Hardness of heart	*Exod 7:20–12:30*
Rebellion	*Num 16:1–44*

God's own purposes   *Job 1:1–2:6; 42:10–17*

CALEB
God-fearing spy   *Num 13:1–2, 6, 26–30*
Honored by God   *Num 14:24, 30, 36–38*
Received land in Canaan   *Josh 14:6–15*

CALF
Offered in sacrifice   *Lev 9:2–3; Mic 6:6*
Aaron's golden idol   *Exod 32:1–6*

CALLING *(See also Career, Election)*
Obedience to one's   *1 Cor 7:17–24*
From God   *Rom 8:30; 11:29*
High, holy, heavenly   *Phil 3:14; 2 Tim 1:9; Heb 3:1*
Goals of it   *Rom 8:30; 1 Cor 7:15; Gal 5:13*

CALVARY *(See also Crucifixion, Jesus Christ)*
Place where Christ was crucified   *Matt 27:33*

CANA
Where Christ turned water into wine   *John 2:1–11*

CANAAN
The land and God's promise   *Gen 10:19, Exod 3:8*
Its peoples   *Exod 3:17*
God's promises concerning   *Gen 15:16–21; 26:2–4*

CANAANITES
Cursed descendants of Ham   *Gen 9:25–26*

Idolatrous and wicked   *Lev 18:24–27; Deut 29:17–18*
Destroyed in judgment   *Exod 23:23–33; Judg 1:1–36*
Communion with Israel forbidden   *Deut 7:2–3*

CAPERNAUM

Christ's healing there:

A centurion's servant   *Matt 8:5–13*
Peter's mother-in-law and others   *Mark 1:21–34*
A paralytic   *Mark 2:1–12*
A nobleman's son   *John 4:46–54*

CAPTIVITY *(See also Bondage, Liberty, Servant)*

Of Israel:

In Egypt, foretold   *Gen 15:13–14*
In Egypt, fulfilled   *Exod 1:1–14*
In Assyria and Babylon, foretold   *Amos 7:11; Isa 39:6*
In Assyria and Babylon, fulfilled   *2 Kings 17:3–24;*
                                              24:10–25:21
Because of idolatry and disobedience   *Deut 28:36–38;*
                                               Amos 5:25–27

Symbolic of being:

Under Satan   *2 Tim 2:26*
In need of Christ   *Luke 4:18*

CARE *(See also Anxiety, Stress, Worry)*

Of believers for one another   *1 Cor 12:25*
Casting on Christ   *1 Pet 5:7*
Christ's rebuke of Martha's   *Luke 10:41*
Of man in need   *Luke 10:34*
Reproof of anxiety   *Phil 4:6*

CAREER *(See also Business, Vocation)*

Commit to the Lord	*Prov 16:3*
Serve the Lord in	*Col 3:23–25*

Showing good will:

In service as to God	*Eph 6:7*
As employee	*Eph 6:8*
As employer	*Eph 6:9*

CARMEL, MOUNT

Hiding from God on	*Amos 9:3*
By the sea	*Jer 46:18*
Showdown at	*1 Kings 18:19*
David weds Abigail of	*1 Sam 25:40*
Elijah at	*2 Kings 4:25*

CELEBRATION *(See Dancing, Feast)*

CELIBACY *(See also Asceticism, Marriage)*

Paul wishes it for all men	*1 Cor 7:7*
Benefit of remaining in	*1 Cor 7:8*
Not a command from the Lord	*1 Cor 7:25*
Though married	*1 Cor 7:29*
Conducive to service	*1 Cor 7:32*

CHANGE *(See also Corruption, Instability, Steadfastness)*

God does not	*Mal 3:6*
Of believers at resurrection	*1 Cor 15:51–52*
Of believers into the Lord's likeness	*2 Cor 3:18*
Of believers' bodies to glorious bodies	*Phil 3:21*

CHARACTER *(See also Growth, Integrity, Virtue)*

List of good qualities	2 Pet 1:5–7
Of a leader	Titus 1:7–9
Security of	Prov 10:9
Which is controlled	Prov 16:32
Boldness of	Esther 4:16
Fickleness of	Luke 22:60–62

CHARITY *(See also Beneficence, Benevolence, Love)*

Need to sustain the poor	Lev 25:35
Blessings on those who practice	Ps 41:1
Happiness for those who practice	Prov 14:21
Required by Jesus	Matt 19:21
Demonstrated by Paul	Gal 2:10

CHASTISEMENT *(See also Chiding, Discipline, Reproof)*

Training by	Heb 12:11
For those God loves	Heb 12:6
Not to be despised	Prov 3:11

CHASTITY *(See also Celibacy, Purity)*

Of wives	1 Pet 3:2
Is will of God	1 Thess 4:3, 7

CHERUBIM *(See also Angels, Seraphim)*

In the tabernacle	Exod 25:20
In the temple	1 Kings 6:23–28
In Ezekiel's vision	Ezek 41:17–20, 25

CHIDING *(See also Chastisement, Discipline)*

Of Israelites by Moses	*Exod 17:2*
Of the Lord	*Ps 103:9*
By Martha	*Luke 10:40*

CHIEF PRIEST *(See also Priest)*

Office instituted	*Lev 21:10–15*
Garments of	*Exod 28:2–42*
Duties of	*Heb 5:1–4*
Christ as	*Heb 4:14–16*
Delivered Jesus to Pilate	*Matt 27:1–2*

CHILDREN *(See also Baby, Family)*

To obey parents	*Col 3:20*
Of God:	
Power to become	*John 1:12*
Spirit bears witness that we are	*Rom 8:16*
Symbolic:	
Becoming as	*Matt 18:2*
In understanding	*1 Cor 14:20*

CHOICE *(See also Acting Wisely, Decision, Opportunity)*

God made	*Acts 15:7; Eph 1:4–5; 1 Thess 1:4*
Of Stephen	*Acts 6:5*
Of Moses	*Ps 106:23*

CHRIST *(See also Jesus Christ)*

Is the Son of God	*Matt 16:16*
Needed to suffer	*Luke 26:26*
Demonstrated his love	*Rom 5:8*

Is end of Law   *Rom 10:4*
Is proclaimed   *Phil 1:18*
Worth of knowing   *Phil 3:8*
Righteousness through faith in   *Rom 3:22*

CHRISTIAN *(See also Conversion, Disciple)*
How to become   *John 3:16*
Characteristics of   *John 13:34–35; Gal 5:22–24*
Suffering as   *1 Pet 4:16*
First called   *Acts 11:26*

CHRISTMAS *(See also Birth, Incarnation, Nativity)*
Observance of Christ's birth   *Matt 1:18–2:11*
Observance of God coming in flesh   *1 Tim 3:16*

CHURCH *(See also Assembly, Body)*
Building of   *Matt 16:18; Eph 2:20–21*
Head of   *Eph 1:22*
Loved by Christ   *Eph 5:25*
Persecuted by Paul   *Gal 1:13*
The pillar and bulwark of truth   *1 Tim 3:15*
Gifts of   *1 Cor 12:27–30*

CIRCUMCISION
A sign of covenant   *Gen 17:10*
Not required for Gentile converts   *Acts 15:1–21*
Faith replaces   *Gal 5:6*
A matter of the heart   *Rom 2:28–29*

CITIZENSHIP *(See also Authority, Society)*

Obligations of	*Rom 13:1–17; 1 Pet 2:13–17*
Punishment for neglect of	*Ezra 7:26*
Jesus discussed	*Matt 17:24–27; 22:17–21*

CLEANSING *(See also Atonement, Sanitation, Washing)*
Figurative of:

Forgiveness of sin	*Ps 51:7, 10; 1 John 1:7*

CLEOPAS

A disciple	*Luke 24:18*

CLOTHING

Figurative of unrighteousness	*Isa 64:6*
Of women	*1 Tim 2:9–10; 1 Pet 3:3–4*
Ceremonial cleansing of	*Lev 11:32*

CLOUD

Rainbow in	*Gen 9:13–16*
Pillar of	*Exod 13:21–22*
Likening love to	*Hos 6:4*
Christ returning in	*Luke 21:27*

COLOSSE

Paul's letter to the church at	*Col 1:1–4:18*

COMFORT *(See also Comforter, Consolation)*

Given to Job	*Job 2:11*
For God's people	*Isa 40:1*

In bereavement   *John 11:19*
In Christ   *Phil 2:1*

COMFORTER *(See also Comfort, Holy Spirit)*

Jesus promised   *John 14:16*
Is the Holy Spirit   *John 14:17*
Is teacher of all things   *John 14:26*
Convicts of sin   *John 16:8*
Is a guide   *John 16:13*
Brings glory to Christ   *John 16:14*

COMMANDMENTS *(See also Law, Ten Commandments)*

Of God   *John 15:12*
Of Jesus:
Examples of   *Matt 5:16, 27–28, 31–32, 34*
Of a father   *Prov 6:20; 7:1*

COMMERCE *(See also Business, Finances, Work)*

Misuse of   *Matt 21:12–13*
Use of money from   *Luke 19:8*
Converts engaged in   *Acts 16:17; 18:2–3*
Cheating in   *Hos 12:7*

COMMUNION *(See also Eucharist, Loaf, Lord's Supper)*

Instituted by Christ   *1 Cor 11:23–26*
Signified by bread and wine   *1 Cor 10:16–17*
Christ's death proclaimed by   *1 Cor 11:26*
Examining of heart before   *1 Cor 11:27–29*

Early church observed   *Acts 2:42*

COMMUNION OF SAINTS *(See also Fellowship, Unity)*

In early church	*Acts 2:42*
Thanks for	*Phil 1:5*
In Christ's love	*Phil 2:1–2*
With God and Jesus Christ	*John 17:21; 1 John 1:3*
When walking in light	*1 John 1:6–7*

COMPASSION *(See also Beneficence, Kindness, Pity)*

Of God	*Deut 13:17; Ps 78:38*
Of Jesus	*Matt 9:36*
Of Good Samaritan	*Luke 10:33–34*
As a mark of believers	*1 Pet 3:8*

COMPLAINING *(See also Frustration, Impatience)*

No need for	*Ps 144:14–15*
Against God	*Job 7:13–14*
Bitterness of	*Job 23:2*
Poured out to God	*Ps 102:1–11*
Of the Jews against Paul	*Acts 25:7*

COMPROMISE *(See also Diplomacy)*

Encouraged for one's own good	*Prov 25:8–10*
In reconciliation	*Matt 5:24–25*

CONCEIT *(See also Arrogance, Boasting, Pride)*

Attributed to fools	*Prov 26:5*
One who has is hopeless	*Prov 26:12*

Attributed to the lazy   Prov 26:16
Not to characterize Christians   Rom 12:16
Dangers of   1 Tim 3:6

CONDEMNATION *(See also Punishment, Wrath)*

Of man   John 3:19
Remedy for   John 5:24
Resulted from Adam's sin   Rom 5:16
None for those in Christ   Rom 8:1
Of Sodom and Gomorrah   2 Pet 2:6

CONDUCT *(See also Behavior, Guidance)*

Of an elder   1 Tim 3:2–7
Of a deacon   1 Tim 3:8–10
Of wives   Prov 31:10–31; 1 Tim 3:11; Titus 2:3–5
Of older men   Titus 2:2
Of younger men   Titus 2:6–7

CONFESSION

That Jesus is Lord   Rom 10:9–10; Phil 2:11
That Jesus is the Son of God   1 John 4:15
Of sins to God   1 John 1:9
To one another   James 5:16
Of evil practices   Acts 19:18
Of Christ before others   Matt 10:32–33

CONFIDENCE *(See also Boldness, Courage, Trust)*

In the Son of God   1 John 5:14–15
In God   1 Pet 1:21
Misplaced   Mic 7:5

53

In self   *Phil 3:4–8*

CONFUSION
None with God   *1 Cor 14:33*
Of language at Babel   *Gen 11:6–9*
God drove enemies into   *Exod 23:27*
Jerusalem in   *Acts 21:31*

CONSCIENCE
Affirmation of a good   *Acts 23:1*
Maintaining a clear   *Acts 24:16*
Bears witness to God   *Rom 2:15*
Of the weaker brother   *2 Cor 8:12*
Maintains truth   *1 Tim 3:9*
Cleansed by Christ   *Heb 9:14*

CONSECRATION *(See also Dedication, Holiness, Sanctification)*
Of priests   *Exod 29:1–46*
Of Christ   *Heb 10:20*
Of believers   *Rom 12:1–2; 2 Cor 8:5*

CONSIDERATION *(See also Kindness)*
To the poor   *Ps 41:1; Prov 29:7*
Of sin   *Ezek 18:28*

CONSOLATION *(See also Comfort, Compassion)*
Attribute of God   *Rom 15:5*
In Christ   *Phil 2:1*
Of Paul   *Philem 7*

Of Israel   *Luke 2:25*

CONTENTMENT *(See also Anxiety, Peace)*

With what one has   *Heb 13:5*
In any situation   *Phil 4:11*
Of mind   *Isa 26:3*
In believing in Christ   *Rom 15:13*
Through walking by the Spirit   *Gal 5:22*

CONVERSATION *(See also Mouth, Speech, Tongue)*

Should be honest   *1 Pet 2:12*
Should be edifying   *Eph 4:29–5:4*
Should be gracious   *Col 4:6*

CONVERSION *(See also Regeneration, Repentance)*

Of sinners:
Turned from idols   *1 Thess 1:9*
Become new creatures   *2 Cor 5:17*
Comes from God through Christ   *2 Cor 5:18–19*
Repentance needed for   *Acts 2:38*
Of Paul   *Acts 9:22, 26*
Of Gentiles   *Acts 15:3*

CONVICTION OF SIN *(See also Guilt, Remorse, Sin)*

The Law brings   *Rom 2:15*
The Holy Spirit brings   *John 16:7–8*
Through Peter's sermon   *Acts 2:37*
Comes from God   *Job 33:27–30*

CORINTH
Apollos visited   *Acts 11:1*
Paul's contact with:
Travelled to   *Acts 18:1*
Wrote the church there   *1 Cor 1:2*
Did not visit again   *2 Cor 1:23–2:4*

CORNELIUS
His vision and call for Peter   *Acts 10:1–8*
Peter's sermon at his house   *Acts 10:34–48*

CORNERSTONE *(See also Foundation)*
Figuratively, Christ is the   *Matt 21:42; Eph 2:20*

CORRUPTION *(See also Disease, Health, Sickness)*
Christ's flesh did not see   *Acts 2:31*
Creation will be freed from   *Rom 8:21*
Of the world   *2 Pet 1:4*

COUNSEL
Of the wicked   *Ps 1:1; Prov 12:5*
Of the Lord   *Ps 16:7; Isa 28:29*
Accepted by the wise   *Prov 12:15; 19:20*
Rejecting God's   *Prov 1:28–30*
A Christian's role to give   *Rom 15:14*

COURAGE *(See also Boldness, Confidence)*
Call to   *Deut 31:7; Josh 1:6–9; Ps 27:14*
From seeing friends   *Acts 28:15*
Paul testified to having   *2 Cor 5:6–8*

COURTS

Instructions regarding	*Exod 23:1–8*
Justice required of	*Deut 1:16–17*
Abiding by sentence of	*Deut 17:8–12*

COVENANT *(See also Promise, Vow)*

Between God and Noah	*Gen 9:12–15*
Between God and Abraham	*Gen 17:1–8*
Between God and the Israelites	*Exod 19:3–6*
Christ brought a new one	*Heb 8:6–13; 10:18; 12:24*

COVETOUSNESS *(See also Avarice, Envy, Greed)*

Against God's decree	*Exod 20:17*
Jesus' instruction against	*Luke 12:15*
Against Paul's teaching	*Col 3:5*

COWARDICE *(See also Courage, Fear)*

Shown by:

Israel's spies	*Num 13:30–31*
Jonah	*Jon 1:1–3*
Pilate	*John 19:12–16*
Peter	*John 18:15–18*

CREATION *(See also Earth, World)*

Account of	*Gen 1:1–2:25*
Work of the Lord	*Ps 104:1–35*
Work of the Word	*John 1:1–14*
Work of the Son	*Col 1:13–17; Heb 1:1–3*

57

CREATIVITY *(See also Art)*

Used for God's purposes	*Gen 35:4–38:23*

CRIME *(See also Law, Sin, Ten Commandments)*

Murder of Abel	*Gen 4:8–9*
Selling of Joseph	*Gen 37:26–28*
Murder of Abner	*2 Sam 3:22–29*
Deceit of Ananias and Sapphira	*Acts 5:1–6*
Cheating of Zaccheus	*Luke 19:1–8*

CROSS *(See also Atonement, Crucifixion, Redemption)*

Bearing of	*John 19:17*
Death on	*Mark 15:22–26; John 19:16–37*
Prediction of	*John 3:14–15*

CROWN *(See also King)*

Literal:

Worn by the high priest	*Lev 8:9*
Worn by the kings	*2 Sam 12:30*

Figurative:

Of a virtuous woman	*Prov 12:4*
Of children	*Prov 17:6*

Rewards:

For the Apostle Paul	*Phil 4:1*
For adherence to principles	*2 Tim 2:5*

CRUCIFIXION *(See also Atonement, Redemption, Resurrection)*

Literal:

Prediction	*Matt 20:29; John 12:32*

Time of	*John 19:14*
Event	*Mark 15:22–26; John 19:16–37*
Figurative:	
Union with Christ	*Rom 6:5; Gal 2:20*

CRUELTY *(See also Beating)*

Characteristic of the wicked	*Ps 37:14*
To animals	*Num 22:27–35*
Example of:	
Herod the Great	*Matt 2:13–16*
To the faithful	*Heb 11:35–38*
The Judaizers	*Acts 14:19*

CURIOSITY

Eve and the tree of life	*Gen 3:6*
Zaccheus'	*Luke 19:1–6*
Jews' questioning of John the Baptist	*John 1:19–27*
Athenians'	*Acts 17:21*

CURSE *(See also Damnation, Oath)*

On Cain's farming	*Gen 4:11–13*
On Israel's disobedience	*Deut 28:15–45*
On Jericho's rebuilders	*Josh 6:26*
Jesus' on the fig tree	*Mark 11:12–14, 20–21*

CYRUS

King of Persia	*2 Chron 36:22*
Prophecies concerning	*Isa 44:28; 45:1*

D

DAMARIS
Young woman who followed Paul   *Acts 17:34*

DAMASCUS
Abraham's journey	*Gen 14:15*
David's victory	*2 Sam 8:5–6*
In Paul's life:	
Journey to	*Acts 9:1–9*
Conversion at	*Acts 9:10–19*
Escapes from	*2 Cor 11:32–33*

DAMNATION *(See also Curse, Punishment)*
For blasphemy against the Holy Spirit	*Mark 3:29*
Against Scribes and Pharisees	*Matt 23:14*
Of:	
Faithless	*Rom 14:23*
Evil doers	*Rom 3:8*
Resurrected	*John 5:29*

DAN
Son of Jacob	*Gen 30:6*
Blessed by Jacob	*Gen 49:16*
Tribe idolatrous	*Judg 18:30; 1 Kings 12:29*

DANCING
By worshipers	*Ps 149:3*
By children	*Matt 11:16–17*

Because of victory over enemies   *1 Sam 18:6–7*
Because of son's return   *Luke 15:22–25*
By daughter of Herodias   *Matt 14:6*

DANGER
Spiritual neglect is   *Heb 2:1–3*
Examples of:
Jesus and the disciples at sea   *Luke 8:22–25*
Paul's perilous voyage   *Acts 27:9–44*
Paul's afflictions   *2 Cor 11:23–33*
Paul's escape from   *Acts 9:22–25*

DANIEL *(See also Prophecy, Prophet)*
Taken to Babylon   *Dan 1:1–7*
Interpreted dreams   *Dan 2:1–45*
Interpreted handwriting   *Dan 5:10–29*
Honored by rulers   *Dan 2:46–49; 6:1–3, 23–28*
Cast into the lion's den   *Dan 6:6–22*
Saw visions   *Dan 7:1–14*

DARIUS
Became king of Babylon   *Dan 5:30–31*
Had Daniel put in lion's den   *Dan 6:16*
Decreed worship of Daniel's God   *Dan 6:25–27*

DARKNESS *(See also Blindness, Light)*
Before the world existed   *Gen 1:2–4*
The plague of   *Exod 10:21–22*
The righteous as light in   *Ps 112:4*
At the death of Christ   *Matt 27:45*

Fruitless deeds of   *Eph 5:11*

DAUGHTER *(See also Family, Son)*

The ideal   *Prov 31:29*
A loyal   *Ruth 1:12–18*
A beautiful   *Ps 45:9–13*

DAVID

Genealogy of   *1 Chron 2:3–15*
Shepherd   *1 Sam 16:11–12*
Slayer of Goliath   *1 Sam 17:4, 49*
Chosen of God   *1 Sam 16:1, 13*
King over Judah, Israel   *2 Sam 2:1–4, 11; 5:1–5*
Faith of   *Heb 11:32–33*

DAY *(See also Night)*

Creation of   *Gen 1:5, 16*
Of the Lord   *Jer 45:10; 1 Thess 5:2*
Symbol of the present age   *Heb 1:2*

DEACON *(See also Elder, Servant)*

Ordination by the apostles   *Acts 6:1–6*
Listed with the elders   *Phil 1:1*
Qualifications of   *1 Tim 3:8–13*
Phoebe a female   *Rom 16:1*

DEAD SEA

Salt sea   *Num 34:3, 12*
Sea of the Plain   *Deut 3:17*
South boundary of Judah   *Josh 15:2, 5*

DEAFNESS

Protection of the Lord	*Lev 19:14*
Healing by the Lord	*Matt 11:5; Mark 7:37*

Spiritual:

Of man	*Ps 38:13*
Of Israel	*Isa 42:18*

DEATH *(See also Bereavement, Burial, Mortality)*

Eternal:

Result of God's wrath	*1 Thess 1:10*
Second death	*Rev 20:14*

Natural:

Consequence of sin	*Gen 3:3; Rom 5:12*
Termination of earthly life	*Eccles 9:10*
Return to dust	*Gen 3:19*
Lot of all men	*Heb 9:27*

DEBORAH

Prophetess who judged and delivered Israel	*Judg 4:4–24*
Her song	*Judg 5:1–31*

DEBT, DEBTOR *(See also Money)*

Usury Prohibited	*Deut 23:19–20; Ezek 18:8–17*
Parable of Jesus	*Matt 18:23–35*

Figuratively:

Of sin	*Matt 6:12*
Moral obligation	*Rom 1:14*

DECEIT *(See also Lying)*

The wicked's pleasure	*Prov 20:17*

| Of servants of Satan | 2 Cor 11:14 |
| The sign of the antichrist | 1 John 4:1–6 |

Examples of:

Isaac	Gen 26:7
David	1 Sam 21:12–13
Ananias and Sapphira	Acts 5:1–11

DECISION *(See also Choice, Guidance)*

To believe God	Heb 11:6
To serve the Lord	Josh 24:15
To continue in the faith	1 Cor 16:13, Acts 14:22
To resist the devil	James 4:7
To not follow Christ	Luke 18:18–23

DECREES *(See also Law)*

For teaching	Exod 18:20
That are just and unjust	Prov 8:15; Isa 10:1–2
Resisting	Rom 13:2
Submission to	1 Pet 2:13

DEDICATION *(See also Consecration, Holiness)*

Of the altar	Num 7:1–3
For service	Judg 5:2
Of God's house	2 Chron 2:4
Of lives	Rom 12:1

DEFILEMENT *(See also Apostasy, Sin)*

Ceremonial	Mark 7:1–4
Comes from the heart	Mark 7:14–23
Of deceivers and rebels	Jude 8

DELILAH

Lover of Samson who betrayed him   *Judg 16:4–21*

DELIVERANCE, DIVINE *(See also Bondage,*
Salvation)

God provides   *Ps 32:7; 116:6*
Of apostles from prison   *Acts 5:18–19*
Of Paul from torture   *2 Tim 4:17*
From evil   *Matt 6:13*
Through prayers and the Spirit   *Phil 1:19*

DEMETRIUS

Silversmith   *Acts 19:24*
Disciple   *3 John 12*

DEMON *(See also Devil, Evil, Exorcism)*

Worship of denounced   *Deut 32:16–17; 1 Tim 4:1*
Possession by   *Matt 8:28–34; Mark 7:25–30*
Cast out by Jesus   *Matt 4:24; 8:16*
Cast out by Peter   *Acts 5:16*
Cast out by Paul   *Acts 19:12*
To be punished   *2 Pet 2:4*

DEPENDENCY

On God   *Ps 37:5; 20:7–8; Prov 3:5–6*
Of Paul on the Lord   *1 Cor 4:3–4*
On riches   *Mark 10:23*

DEPRESSION *(See also Anxiety, Despair)*

Counsel concerning, O.T.   *Ps 34:18; 42:11; Zeph 3:17;*

| Counsel concerning, N.T. | Rom 8:31; 12:12 |

Examples of:

David	Ps 22:1–2
Ezra	Ezra 10:1, 6
Peter	Matt 26:75

DESERTION *(See also Abandonment)*

Saved from	Ps 16:10
From the truth by believers	Gal 1:6
Of many disciples	John 6:67

DESIRE *(See also Motive)*

Of God for man	Hos 6:6
For heaven	Heb 11:14
For spiritual gifts	1 Cor 14:1
To accomplish	Prov 13:19
Of the righteous	Prov 10:24
Of the flesh	Gal 5:17; Eph 2:3

DESPAIR

Personal	Num 11:15; Job 10:1
From doing wrong	Luke 22:61–62
Of Jesus	Mark 15:34

DEVIL *(See also Evil, Lucifer, Satan, Serpent)*

Deceived Eve	Gen 3:1–5
Temptation of Jesus by	Matt 4:1–10
Christians to resist	James 4:7

Names of:

| Deceiver, ancient serpent, great dragon | Rev 12:9 |

Angel of light   *2 Cor 11:14*
Beelzebub   *Matt 10:25*

DEVOTION *(See also Dedication, Sanctification)*
To God's will   *Matt 7:21*
Of Christ   *Luke 22:42; 2 Cor 8:9*
To characterize Christians   *Col 1:2*
Between friends   *1 Sam 18:1–3*

DIET *(See also Food)*
Of Daniel   *Dan 1:8–16*
No blood in Israelites'   *Lev 17:12*
Of Nazirite   *Num 6:3–4*

DILIGENCE *(See also Work)*
In obeying   *Zech 6:15*
To be added to faith   *2 Pet 1:5–7*
In behavior   *1 Pet 2:12*

DIPLOMACY *(See also Ambassador, Compromise)*
Of Abigail   *1 Sam 25:28–34*
Of Abraham and Abimelech   *Gen 21:22–23*
Of Paul   *Acts 16:3; 1 Cor 9:20–23*

DISCIPLE *(See also Apostle, Christian, Discipleship)*
Of Jesus   *Matt 10:1–4; Luke 10:1–11*
First called Christians in Antioch   *Acts 11:26*
Known by love for others   *John 13:35*
Bears fruit as proof   *John 15:8*

DISCIPLESHIP *(See also Devotion, Disciple, Growth)*

Responsibility of	*2 Tim 2:2–8*
Characterized by love	*John 21:15–18*
The cost of	*Luke 14:25–33*

DISCIPLINE *(See also Chastisement, Chiding, Reproof)*

By parents	*Prov 19:18; 23:13*
By God	*Heb 12:5–11*

In the church:

Of those who sin	*1 Tim 5:20*
Of restoring one to fellowship	*Gal 6:1*
Of warning the unruly	*1 Tim 6:4–5*
Of false teachers	*1 Tim 6:3*

DISCRETION *(See also Prudence, Tact)*

Of Joseph	*Gen 41:39–40*
In youth	*Prov 5:2*
Desired by David for Solomon	*1 Chron 22:12*

DISEASE *(See also Corruption, Health)*

As judgment	*Num 12:9–10; 2 Chron 21:18*
Inflicted by Satan	*Job 2:7*
Prayer for healing of	*2 Kings 20:3–11*
Healed by Christ	*Matt 4:23; John 5:8–9*
Healed by disciples	*Luke 9:1; Acts 3:2–7*

DISHONESTY *(See also Lying, Treachery)*

Against the poor	*Job 24:3–4; Ezek 22:29*
In business	*Amos 8:5*
Punishment for	*Zeph 1:9; Zech 5:3–4*

DISOBEDIENCE *(See also Obedience, Rebellion)*

To God	*Exod 5:2; 1 Kings 13:21*
To covenant	*Jer 11:3*
To the truth	*Gal 3:1*
Children of	*Eph 5:6*
To the gospel	*2 Thess 1:8*
In neglect of salvation	*Heb 2:3*

DIVORCE *(See also Marriage)*

Jesus' teaching on	*Matt 5:32; 19:9; Mark 10:10–12*
Because of hardness of heart	*Mark 10:5–9*
Paul's view of	*1 Cor 7:27*

DOCTRINE *(See also Law, Teaching)*

For Christian training	*2 Tim 3:16*
Paul's defense of	*Acts 24:14–15*
Warning against false	*Rom 16:17–18*
Of Jesus:	
Came from the Father	*John 7:16–17*
Questioned by high priest	*John 18:19*

DORCAS

Raised from dead by Peter	*Acts 9:40*

DOUBT

In trials	*Mark 4:40; 1 Pet 1:6*
Mixed with faith	*James 1:6–8*
In belief	*John 20:25–29*
Leads to unbelieving heart	*Heb 3:12*

DREAM *(See also Vision)*
Used by God:

To teach	*Gen 28:13–15; Matt 1:20–21*
To warn	*Gen 41:14–32*
To guide	*Matt 2:13*

DRESS *(See Apparel, Clothing)*

DRINKING *(See also Drunkenness, Wine)*

Results of	*Prov 23:21, 29–30, 33–35*
Temperance in	*Eph 5:18*
At wedding	*John 2:3, 9–10*
As an offense to others	*Rom 14:21*

Abstaining from wine:

Priests	*Lev 10:8–10*
Nazirites	*Num 6:3*

DRUNKENNESS *(See also Abstinence from Alcohol, Wine)*

Leads to poverty	*Prov 23:21*
Burdened by	*Luke 21:34*
None in kingdom of God	*1 Cor 6:10*
Is debauchery	*Eph 5:18*

DUTY *(See also Obligation, Responsibility, Servant)*

To worship God	*1 Chron 16:28–30*
To do right in God's sight	*Deut 6:18*
To do good to others	*Prov 3:27*
Of Jesus to God	*Luke 2:49*
To government	*Rom 13:6–7*

To love   *Rom 13:8*

E

EAR
Made by God for listening   *Prov 20:12*
The wise use it for knowledge   *Prov 18:15*
Blessed are those who use it   *Rev 1:3*

EARTH *(See also Creation, world)*
Created by God   *Gen 1:1*
To be inhabited   *Isa 45:13*
God brought judgments on   *Gen 3:14–19*
Supreme authority of   *Matt 28:18*
Vision of a new:
God and his people will be there   *Rev 21:3*
No death and no tears   *Rev 21:4*

EASTER
Sunday commemorating Resurrection   *John 20:1–18*

EDEN
Garden of   *Gen 2:8*
Adam driven from   *Gen 3:24*

EDOM
Land of Esau   *Gen 32:3*
Prophecies concerning   *Isa 34:5; Jer 25:21;*
                                        Ezek 25:13; Amos 1:11

EGYPT *(See also Pharaoh)*

Joseph made a ruler of	*Gen 41:44*
Israel in bondage to	*Exod 1:8–14*
Plagues brought on	*Exod 7:17–11:10*
God delivered Israelites from	*Exod 14:30*

ELDER *(See also Bishop, Deacon)*
Of the church:

Qualifications of	*Titus 1:6–9*
Appointed by local church	*Acts 14:23*
Participates in local church decisions	*Acts 15:6–29*
Willingly leads believers	*1 Peter 5:2–3*
Ministers to the sick	*James 5:14–15*

ELEAZAR

Son of Aaron and chief priest	*Exod 6:23*
Son of Abinadab	*1 Sam 7:1*
One of David's captains	*2 Sam 23:9*

ELECTION *(See also Call, Predestination)*
Of believers:

According to God's call and purpose	*Rom 9:11*
Before the world began	*Eph 1:4*
By grace	*Rom 11:5*
For God's glory	*Eph 1:6*
Through faith	*2 Thess 2:13*

ELI

Trained the boy Samuel	*1 Sam 1:25–28; 2:11*

ELIAKIM

Chief minister of Hezekiah	*2 Kings 18:18–37*

ELIHU

Reproved Job's friends	*Job 32:2–37:24*

ELIJAH

Prophet persecuted by King Ahab	*1 Kings 17:2–3*
Fed by raven	*1 Kings 17:4*
Brought to life widow's son	*1 Kings 17:17–24*
Contest with Baal worshipers	*1 Kings 18:19–40*
Predicted drought	*1 Kings 17:1*
Went to heaven in a whirlwind	*2 Kings 2:11*

ELISHA

Successor to Elijah	*1 Kings 19:16*
Was given Elijah's cloak	*2 Kings 2:13*
Miracles of:	
Brought child back to life	*2 Kings 4:32–35*
Healed Naaman the leper	*2 Kings 5:9–14*

ELIZABETH

Wife of Zechariah	*Luke 1:5*
Childless until old age	*Luke 1:7*
Mother of John the Baptist	*Luke 1:13*
Visited by Mary	*Luke 1:39*
Filled with the Holy Spirit	*Luke 1:41*

EMMAUS

Christ talked to disciples on road to	*Luke 24:15*

EMPLOYEE *(See also Business, Duty, Work)*

Not to be oppressed	*Deut 24:14*
To be paid on time	*Deut 24:15*
Deserves to be paid	*Luke 10:7; 1 Tim 5:18*

EMPLOYER *(See also Employee)*

To pay for services	*Jer 22:13*
Indebted to his workers	*Rom 4:4*
To treat employees justly	*Col 4:1*

ENEMY

Do good to and love	*Luke 6:35*
Help when in trouble	*Exod 23:4–5*
Pray for	*Matt 5:44*
Last to be destroyed	*1 Cor 15:26*
Of the cross	*Phil 3:18–19*

ENOCH

His dedication	*Gen 5:18*
His faith	*Heb 11:5*
Did not die	*Gen 5:24*

ENVY *(See also Contentment, Covetousness, Jealousy)*

Instructed to avoid	*1 Pet 2:1*
Chief priests showed	*Mark 15:10*
Toward the wicked	*Prov 24:19*
Toward the violent	*Prov 3:31*
Leads to evil	*James 3:16*

EPHESUS

Paul's contact with:

Visited twice by Paul	*Acts 18:18–21; 19:1*
Laid hands on disciples	*Acts 19:6*
Spoke in synagogue	*Acts 19:8*
Performed miracles	*Acts 19:11–12*
Where believers gave up magic	*Acts 19:18–19*

EPHRAIM

Second son of Joseph	*Gen 41:52*
Tribe of Israel	*Gen 49:25*
Moses blessed	*Deut 33:13–17*
Worshiped Baal	*Hos 13:1*
Sin noted	*Hos 13:12*

ESAU

Twin son of Isaac and Rebecca	*Gen 25:19–26*
Sold his birthright for food	*Gen 25:29–34*
Cheated out of father's blessing	*Gen 27:30–36*

ESTHER

Raised by Mordecai, her cousin	*Esther 2:7*
Chosen as queen	*Esther 2:17*
Interceded for her people, the Jews	*Esther 8:3–8*

ETERNAL LIFE *(See Life, Salvation)*

ETERNITY *(See also Immortality, Heaven, Hell)*

God inhabits	*Isa 57:15*
God put into man's mind	*Eccles 3:11*

The Lord will reign for	*Exod 15:18*
Believers will live for	*Ps 23:6*
Rewards in	*Matt 19:28–30*
God's promise of life in	*1 John 2:25*

ETHICS *(See also Conduct, Morality)*

Christians obliged to practice	*Prov 14:2; Titus 2:12*
For employers	*Col 4:1*
For employees	*Col 3:23*
For citizens	*Rom 13:1–7*
For God's glory	*Matt 5:16*

ETHIOPIA

Prophecies concerning	*Ps 68:31; Isa 18:20*

EUCHARIST *(See also Communion, Lord's Supper)*

Instituted by Christ	*Matt 26:26–28; Mark 14:22–24*
Observed by early church	*Acts 2:42, 46*
Preparing for	*1 Cor 11:27–29*

EUNICE

Mother of Timothy	*2 Tim 1:5*

EUTYCHUS

Young man raised from dead by Paul	*Acts 20:7–12*

EVANGELISM *(See also Gospel, Witness, Mission)*

Some believers have gift of	*Eph 4:11*
Paul charged Timothy to do	*2 Tim 4:5*
Of Paul to the Gentiles	*Eph 3:8*

To be worldwide   *Mark 13:10*

EVE *(See also Adam, Fall of Man)*
Created by God   *Gen 2:20–23*
Deceived by serpent   *Gen 3:1–7*
Curse pronounced on   *Gen 3:16*
Children of   *Gen 4:1–2, 25; 5:3–4*

EVIL *(See also Abomination, Motive, Sin)*
Source of   *Gen 3:1–6*
God's attitude toward   *Rom 1:18*
Doers of   *Ps 37:1–2*
Examples of   *1 Sam 19:1, 10; Rom 1:29–31*
Returned for good   *1 Sam 25:21*
Turning from   *Jer 18:8*
Appearance of   *1 Thess 5:22*

EXODUS *(See also Moses, Red Sea)*
Israel's deliverance from Egypt   *Exod 12:41–42*
Led by Moses   *Exod 3:7–10; Acts 7:20–36*

EXORCISM *(See also Deliverance, Demon)*
Practiced by Christ   *Matt 8:16*
Power given disciples   *Matt 10:1*
Attempted by others   *Acts 19:13*

EYE *(See also Vision)*
Of the Lord   *Ps 33:18; Amos 9:8*
Lust of   *1 John 2:16*
Lamp of body   *Luke 11:34*

EZEKIEL

Priest in Babylonian exile	*Ezek 1:1–13*
Saw God's glory in a vision	*Ezek 1:26–28*
Called son of man	*Ezek 2:1*
Prophesied to rebellious Israel	*Ezek 2:3–5*
Acted out the coming destruction	*Ezek 4:1–8*

EZRA

Scribe and priest	*Ezra 7:11*
Spoke against marriage to heathen	*Ezra 10:10–11*
Read the law to the people	*Ezra 8:2–3*
Commissioned by King of Persia:	
To lead group of Jews to Jerusalem	*Ezra 7:12–13*
To carry treasures to temple	*Ezra 7:15–16*

F

FACE *(See also Anthropomorphism)*

Of God	*Ex 33:23*
Of Christ	*Matt 17:2*
Representing God's look:	
Of favor	*Num 6:25*
Of disfavor	*Ps 34:16*

FAILURE *(See also Despair, Shame)*

Prayer to prevent	*Luke 22:32*

FAITH *(See also Belief, Witness)*

Gift of God	*Eph 2:8*

Condition of salvation	Acts 16:31
Way of life	Eph 6:16
Author of	Heb 12:2
Object of	John 14:1
Trial of	James 1:3

FAITHFULNESS (See also Steadfastness, Long-suffering)

Seen in God	Lam 3:233; 1 Cor 10:13
Required in believers	Rev 2:10
In service	1 Cor 4:2
In all things	Luke 16:10

FALL OF MAN (See also Sin)

Through Satan's tempting	Gen 3:1–5
Man's state as a result	Rom 3:23
Remedy for, only in Christ	Eph 2:1–8

FAMILY (See also Brother, Father, Mother)

| Established before the Fall | Gen 2:23–24 |

Responsibilities of:

Wives	Col 3:18; Prov 31:11–15
Husbands	Col 3:19
Children	Col 3:20
Fathers	Col 3:21
Mothers	Prov 31:15, 27–28

FAMINE (See also Agriculture, Food)

| Pharaoh warned of in dreams | Gen 41:1–40 |
| Experienced spiritually | 2 Chron 15:3; Amos 8:11 |

Caused by:

Enemies	*Deut 28:49–51; 2 Kings 6:24–25*
Insects	*Joel 1:4*
Hail storms	*Exod 9:23, 31*
Sin	*Ezek 14:12–13*

Occurred in time of:

Abraham	*Gen 12:10*
Isaac	*Gen 26:1*
David	*2 Sam 21:1*
Early Church	*Acts 11:28*

FARMING *(See also Agriculture)*

Introduced by God	*Gen 2:15*
Illustrations, parables based on	*Matt 13:3–8*

FASTING *(See also Asceticism, Food)*

Jesus teaching on	*Matt 6:16–18; Matt 9:15*
For special needs	*Acts 14:23*
Accompanied by prayer	*Acts 13:3*
Not merely as a form	*Isa 58:5–7*

FATHERHOOD *(See also Motherhood)*

Of God to all he created	*Deut 32:6*
Of God to all who believe in his Son	*Gal 4:4–6*
Of God to Jesus Christ	*Col 1:3*

FATIGUE *(See also Sleep, Stress)*

Examples of:

Christ and disciples	*Mark 6:30–31*
Christ en route to the cross	*Luke 23:26*

Help from the Lord in   *Isa 40:31*

FEAR *(See also Anxiety, Worry)*
Reverential, in worship to God   *Heb 12:28*
Commanded of all   *Ps 33:8*
As beginning of wisdom   *Job 28:28*
Dread of future   *Prov 10:24; Luke 21:26*

FEAST
At a wedding   *John 2:1–10*
Given by kings   *Esther 1:3*
At a coronation   *1 Chron 12:38–39*
On occasion of national deliverance   *Esther 8:17*
Parable of   *Luke 14:7–13*

FELIX
Governor of Judea   *Acts 23:23*
Paul's defense before   *Acts 24:10*
Convicted by preaching, but didn't
    release Paul   *Acts 24:24–27*

FELLOWSHIP *(See also Communion of Saints, Unity)*
With God:
For those who love him   *John 14:23*
For those who obey him   *1 John 3:24*
With Christ:
For those gathered in his name   *Matt 18:20*
Of the Holy Spirit:
For those who belong to Christ   *Rom 8:9*

FESTIVAL *(See Feast)*

FESTUS
Governor of Judea after Felix	*Acts 24:27*
Paul's trial before	*Acts 25:6–12*

FIGHTING *(See also Quarrel, Strife)*
Contending for the faith	*1 Tim 6:12*
Against afflictions	*2 Cor 7:5*

FINANCES *(See also Commerce, Money)*
Cheating in	*Amos 8:4–6*
Preparation in	*1 Cor 16:1–2*
Sharing in	*2 Cor 9:7*

FIRE *(See also Judgment)*
Represents:
Cleansing	*Isa 6:6–7*
Spiritual power	*Matt 3:11*
Judgment	*Rev 20:9*
Everlasting punishment	*Mark 9:48*

FIRSTBORN *(See also Birthright, Inheritance)*
Consecrated to God	*Exod 13:2*
Death of	*Exod 11:5*
Christ described as	*Col 1:15*

FIRSTFRUITS *(See also Offering)*
Of harvest:
Required as offering	*Exod 22:29*

As wave offering   *Lev 23:20*
As thank offering on entering Promised Land   *Deut 26:1–4*

FISH
Created   *Gen 1:20–22*
Jonah swallowed by   *Jon 1:17*
Big catch of   *Luke 5:4–9*
Used in miracle   *Matt 14:19*

FLATTERY *(See also Honesty, Mouth)*
Description of those who engage in it   *Ps 5:9*
Purpose condemned   *Jude 16*
Used to pressure   *Prov 7:21*
Related to condition of heart   *Ps 12:2*
Results of   *Prov 26:28*

FLESH *(See also Body, Sin, Spirit)*
Physical man   *Gen 2:23–24*
Represents sinful nature of man   *Eph 2:3*
Works against the Spirit   *Gal 5:17*
Desires of, results in   *Gal 5:19–21*
Christ took form of   *John 1:14*

FOOD *(See also Diet, Drinking, Feast)*
Provided by God for man   *Gen 1:29–30*
For strength and satisfaction   *Ps 104:15*
To abstain from   *Gen 2:16–17*
Disciples concerned about   *Matt 14:15–17*
Christ provided through miracle   *Matt 14:19–20*
Christ gave thanks for   *Mark 8:6*

FOOLISHNESS

Seen by God	Ps 69:5
Of a child	Prov 22:15
Results of	Prov 19:3
As sin	Prov 24:9

To unbelievers:

Preaching of Cross is	1 Cor 1:18
Things of God are	1 Cor 2:14

FOREIGNER

Those who don't understand	1 Cor 14:11
One who thanked Jesus	Luke 17:18
Figuratively, believers no longer are	Eph 3:19

FORGIVENESS *(See also Reconciliation, Redemption, Repentance)*

Of man's sin:

By God	Ps 130:4
By Christ	Acts 10:43
Among believers	Eph 4:32
Of enemies	Luke 6:27

FORMALISM *(See also Pharisees)*

Vain worship	Isa 29:13
Denounced by Christ	Matt 15:7–9
In the last days	2 Tim 3:5

FORNICATION *(See also Adultery, Immorality, Lust)*

Forbidden by God	Exod 20:14
Punishment for	Lev 20:10; Heb 13:4

Christians to abstain from   *1 Thess 4:3*

FOUNDATION *(See also Steadfastness, Stone)*
Of the world:
  Laid by God   *Job 38:4*
  It is firm   *2 Tim 2:19*
  No other but Christ   *1 Cor 3:11*
  Building on it   *1 Cor 3:12–14*

FRIENDSHIP *(See also Affection, Fellowship, Hospitality)*
  Betrayal in   *Ps 41:9*
  Agreement necessary in   *Amos 3:3*
  A continuing relationship   *Prov 17:17*
With God:
  For those who fear him   *Ps 25:14*
Warnings against:
  With the angry   *Prov 22:24*
  With the world   *James 4:4*

FRUIT OF THE SPIRIT *(See also Growth)*
  Described   *Gal 3:23–24*

FRUSTRATION *(See also Impatience)*
Examples of:
  Jesus' expression of   *Matt 23:37*
  Paul's expression of   *Rom 7:15–25*

G

GABRIEL *(See also Angels)*
Angel who appeared:

To Daniel	*Dan 9:21*
To Zacharias	*Luke 1:11–20*
To Mary	*Luke 1:26–28*

GAD

Jacob's son	*Gen 30:11*
Tribe blessed by Moses	*Deut 33:20*
Commended by Joshua	*Josh 22:1*
Charged with idolatry	*Josh 22:11*
Their defense	*Josh 22:21*

GALILEE

District in Israel	*Matt 2:22*
City of refuge in	*Josh 20:7*
Prophecy of	*Isa 9:1*
Herod, king of	*Mark 6:21*
Disciples from	*Acts 1:11*
Jesus taught and healed in	*Matt 4:23*

GAMALIEL

Paul brought up at feet of	*Acts 22:3*
Advised the council	*Acts 5:34*

GATES *(See also Wall)*

Of cities	*Deut 3:5*

Place for:
  Meetings   *Neh 8*
  Judging offenses   *Deut 21:19–20*
  Business   *Gen 23:10*
Figurative:
  Of righteousness   *Ps 118:19*
  Of heaven   *Gen 28:17*
  Of death   *Job 38:17*

GATH

  City of Philistia   *1 Sam 17:4*
  Home of Goliath   *1 Sam 17:4*

GAZA

  Samson carried away gates of   *Judg 16:1–3*
  Destruction foretold   *Jer 47:1–7; Amos 1:6*

GENEALOGY *(See also Ancestor)*

  Of Jesus Christ   *Matt 1:1–16*
  Of the Jews   *Ezra 7:1–5; 8:1–15; Neh 7; 11:12*
  Endless speculating on   *1 Tim 1:4*

GENEROSITY *(See also Beneficence, Liberality)*

  Of God   *Ps 103:3–12*
  Command regarding   *Matt 5:42*
  Example of   *Prov 31:20*

GENTILE *(See also Foreigner, Jew)*

  Guilty of sin   *Rom 2:14–15*
  Salvation available to   *Rom 1:16*

Paul, an apostle to	*Acts 21:19*
Message of salvation preached to	*Acts 28:28*
Became fellow members of church	*Eph 3:6*
No distinction between Jew and	*Gal 3:28*

GENTLENESS *(See Humility, Kindness, Tolerance)*

Of Christ	*2 Cor 10:1*
Deal with others in spirit of	*1 Cor 4:21*
Restoring fellow-believers in spirit of	*Gal 6:1*
A characteristic God likes	*1 Pet 3:4*

GETHSEMANE

Garden of Christ's agony	*Matt 26:36; Luke 22:39*

GIDEON

Angel appeared to	*Judg 6:11*
Lord called to deliver Israel	*Judg 6:14*
Replaced Baal altar with one to the Lord	*Judg 6:26–27*
Prayed for signs of assurance	*Judg 6:36–40*
Delivered Israelites from Midianites	*Judg 8:22*
Declined being king	*Judg 8:23*
Faith of	*Heb 11:32*

GIFT *(See Calling, Generosity)*
Of eternal life:

From God	*John 3:16*
In Christ	*Rom 6:23*
Of Holy Spirit	*Luke 11:13*
Of faith	*Eph 2:8*
Given to each believer	*1 Cor 12:4–11*

Comes from Father   *James 1:17*
Good stewards of   *1 Pet 4:10*

GILEAD
Land granted to Reubenites   *Num 32:1–30*
Invaded by Ammonites   *Judg 10:17*

GILGAL
Joshua camped there   *Josh 4:19; 9:6*
Saul made king there   *1 Sam 10:8; 11:14*
Saul sacrificed there   *1 Sam 13:8; 15:12*

GLORY *(See also Majesty, Presence of God)*
Of God   *Exod 24:5–17; 40:34; Luke 2:9; Acts 7:55*
Of Christ   *John 12:41; 17:5; Luke 9:32; 1 Tim 3:16*
Of temporal things   *Matt 4:8; 1 Thess 2:6; 1 Pet 1:24*
Of believers:
By the Spirit   *2 Cor 3:18*
By Christ's work   *Heb 2:9–10*
Greatness of   *Rom 8:18*
Of God's, reflected:
In Christ   *John 1:14*
In man   *1 Cor 11:7*

GLUTTONY
Warned against   *Prov 23:1–3*
Attribute of the wicked   *Phil 3:19*
Leads to poverty   *Prov 23:21*
Jesus accused of   *Matt 11:19*

GOD *(See also Jesus Christ, Holy Spirit)*

Characteristics of:

Omnipotence	*Jer 32:17, 27*
Omnipresence	*Ps 139:7–12*
Omniscience	*Amos 9:2–3*
Foreknowledge	*Isa 48:3–5*

Moral Characteristics of:

Impartiality	*1 Pet 1:17*
Love	*1 John 4:8*
Mercy	*Lam 3:22–23*
Holiness	*Rev 4:8*
Justice	*Ps 89:14*

Manifestations of:

Voice of	*Deut 5:22–26*
Glory of	*Exod 40:34–35*
In Jesus	*John 14:9*

GOD THE FATHER *(See God)*

GODLINESS *(See also Holiness, Righteousness)*

Response to grace	*Titus 2:11–12*
Value of	*1 Tim 4:8*
As our aim	*1 Tim 6:11*
Wrong view of	*1 Tim 6:5*
A supplement of faith	*2 Pet 1:5–6*

GOLD *(See also Money)*

As money	*Ezra 8:25–28; Ezek 7:19*
Utensils made of	*Exod 25:26, 29, 38, 39*
Figurative	*Prov 17:3; Jer 51:7; 1 Cor 3:12*

Symbolic   *Dan 2:32–45; Rev 21:18–21*

GOLDEN RULE
Given by Jesus   *Matt 7:12; Luke 6:31*

GOMORRAH *(See also Sodom)*
Judged   *Gen 18:20; 19:24, 28; Isa 1:9; Matt 10:15*

GOOD NEWS *(See also Gospel, Evangelism)*
As refreshment   *Prov 15:30; 25:25*
Preached by Paul   *Acts 14:15*

GOODNESS *(See also Righteousness, Virtue)*
Of God:
  To all   *Ps 145:9*
  Abundance of   *Ps 31:19*
  Rejoicing in   *Exod 18:9; 2 Chron 6:41*
  Satisfied with   *Jer 31:14*
Given to those who:
  Fear God   *Ps 31:19*
  Continue in his grace   *Rom 11:22*

GOSHEN
Allotted to Israelites in Egypt   *Gen 45:10; 46:34; 47:4*
No plagues there   *Exod 8:22; 9:26*
Region in Canaan   *Josh 10:41; 11:16*

GOSPEL *(See also Evangelism, Good News, Preaching, Witnessing)*
Of God   *Rom 1:1*

Of Christ	2 Cor 2:12
God's power	Rom 1:16
Source of:	
Hope	Col 1:23
Faith	Acts 15:7
Salvation	2 Thess 2:13–14
Preaching of:	
To the whole creation	Mark 16:15
By Jesus	Mark 1:14–15

GOSSIP *(See also Backbiting, Slander)*

Forbidden under law	Lev 19:16
Consequences of	Prov 16:28
Result of idleness	1 Tim 5:13

GOVERNMENT *(See also Kingdom, Politics, Society)*

Christ's reign	Isa 9:6–7
Christians to:	
Obey	Rom 13:1–7
Pray for	1 Tim 2:1–3

GRACE *(See also Mercy)*

The source of:	
Justification	Rom 3:24
Faith	Acts 18:27
Salvation	Acts 15:11
Forgiveness	Eph 1:7
Descriptions of:	
Sufficient	2 Cor 12:9
Glorious	Eph 1:6

Rich   *Eph 2:7*

GRATITUDE *(See Thankfulness, Ingratitude)*

GREED *(See also Avarice, Covetousness)*
Attributed to false teachers   *2 Pet 2:14*
Results in:
  Betrayal   *Luke 22:1–6*
  Trouble   *Prov 15:27*
  Murder   *1 Kings 21:1–16*
Qualities of:
  Never satisfied   *Eccles 1:8; 5:10*
  Exploits   *2 Pet 2:3*

GRIEF *(See also Comfort, Mourning, Sorrow)*
Attributed to:
  Holy Spirit   *Eph 4:30*
  Suffering servant   *Isa 53:3*
  Jesus   *Mark 3:5*
Results from:
  Hardness of heart   *Mark 3:5*
  Death   *2 Sam 19:1–2*
  Disease   *Job 2:11–13*
  Rebelliousness   *Isa 63:10*

GROWTH *(See also Disciple, Holiness, Sanctification)*
In grace and knowledge of Christ   *2 Pet 3:18*
In Christ-likeness   *Eph 4:13*
In Christ   *Eph 4:15*
Of Jesus in wisdom   *Luke 2:52*

GUIDANCE *(See also Decision, Will of God)*

Continuing	*Isa 58:11*
By God	*Ps 48:14; 73:24*
Need of	*Prov 11:14*
By the Holy Spirit	*Acts 16:6–10*

GUILT *(See also Conviction of Sin, Remorse, Shame)*

A result of sin	*Exod 20:7*
Leads to restoration	*Lev 6:4*
Of uncleanness	*Lev 5:2*
Of all shown through the Law	*Rom 3:19*

H

HABAKKUK

Prophet of God	*Hab 1:1*
Questions of	*Hab 1:2–3, 12–13, 17*
Prayer of	*Hab 3:1–19*

HAGAR

Mother of Ishmael	*Gen 16:3*
Comforted by angel	*Gen 16:10*
Allegory of	*Gal 4:24*

HAGGAI

Prophet of God	*Hag 1:1*
Urged rebuilding of the temple	*Hag 1:1–15*
Rebuked the priests and people	*Hag 2:11–14*

HAIR *(See also Beard)*

Covering of	*1 Cor 11:6–7*
Cutting of	*Lev 19:27; 1 Cor 11:14–15*
Of a Nazirite	*Num 6:5*

Figurative of:

Many	*Ps 40:12*
Respect	*Prov 16:31*
Complete destruction	*Isa 7:20*

HAM

Son of Noah, cursed	*Gen 9:18, 22*
His descendants	*Gen 10:6; 1 Chron 1:8; Ps 105:23*

HAMAN

Official under Xerxes	*Esther 3:1–2*
His sin and fall	*Esther 3:3–10; 7:1–10*

HAND *(See also Anthropomorphism)*

Laying on of	*Acts 6:6; 8:18; 1 Tim 4:14*
Lifting of	*Ps 28:2; 63:4*

God's hand symbolic of:

Omnipotence	*Ps 17:7; 20:6; 44:3*
Miracles	*Exod 3:20*
Protection	*Ps 139:10*
Provision	*Ps 145:16*
Punishment	*Ps 75:8*

HANDICAPPED *(See also Lameness)*

Jesus healed the blind man	*John 9:1–11*
Paul healed the cripple	*Acts 14:8–10*

God will protect the crippled   *Ezek 34:16*

HANNAH
Mother of Samuel   *1 Sam 1:11–19*
Her song   *1 Sam 2:1–10*

HAPPINESS *(See also Contentment, Joy)*
Of the wicked:
Short lived   *Job 20:5*
Unstable   *Luke 20:20*
Temporary   *Luke 16:24–25*
Obtained through:
Trusting God   *Prov 16:20*
Fearing God   *Ps 128:1–2*
Obeying God   *John 13:15–17*

HARP *(See also Music)*
Used:
To drive out evil spirits   *1 Sam 16:16–23*
In worship   *Ps 33:2*
To entertain   *Gen 31:27*
By the wicked   *Isa 5:11–12*
In the temple orchestra   *1 Chron 16:5*
By the prophets   *1 Sam 10:5*

HARVEST *(See also Agriculture, Feast)*
Feast of   *Exod 23:16*
Joy of   *Isa 9:3*
Figurative of:
Judgment   *Jer 51:33; Hos 5:11*

People needing God	Jer 8:20: Matt 9:37–38
World's end	Matt 13:30, 39
Final judgment	Rev 14:15

HATRED *(See also Anger, Malice)*

| A work of the flesh | Gal 5:20 |
| Liable to judgment | Matt 5:22 |

Recipients of:

God	Exod 20:5
Christ	John 15:25
Believers	Matt 5:11; 24:9
Evil doers	Ps 26:5

HEAD *(See also Body)*

Figurative of:

God	1 Cor 11:3
Christ	Eph 1:22
Man	1 Cor 11:3, 7
Pride	Ps 83:2
Confidence	Luke 21:28
Joy	Ps 23:5

HEALTH *(See also Disease, Medicine, Sickness)*

Detriments to:

Sin	Ps 38:3
Wickedness	Ps 55:23
Immorality	Prov 7:22–27

Aids to:

| Obedience | Prov 4:20–22 |
| Food | Acts 27:34 |

Exercise   *1 Tim 4:8*

HEART *(See also Soul)*
Source of:

Actions   *Matt 12:33–35*

Desires   *Rom 10:1*

Obedience   *Rom 6:17*

Sorrow   *John 14:1*

Conditions of:

Pure   *Ps 73:1*

Contrite   *Ps 51:17*

Proud   *Jer 49:16*

Hardened   *Rom 2:5*

Believing   *Rom 10:10*

Loving   *Matt 22:37*

Trusting   *Prov 3:5*

HEATHEN *(See also Unbeliever)*

God rules over   *Ps 47:7–8*

God's goodness to   *Acts 14:17*

Are guilty before God   *Rom 1:18–19*

God wants them to be saved   *Titus 2:11*

Not to be imitated   *Jer 10:2–3; Matt 6:7–8*

Declaring God's glory among   *Ps 96:3*

HEAVEN *(See also Eternity, Hell, Paradise)*
Characteristics of:

No corruption   *1 Cor 15:42, 50*

No pain   *Rev 21:4*

No death   *Luke 20:36*

Joy	*Luke 15:7*
Peace	*Luke 16:25*
Glory	*Rom 8:17–18*
Residents of:	
God	*1 Kings 8:30*
Christ	*Heb 9:12, 24*
Righteous	*Matt 25:34–37*
Angels	*Matt 18:10*

HEBRON

Joshua conquered it	*Josh 10:36*
Capital under David	*2 Sam 2:1; 3:2; 5:1*

HEIR *(See also Birthright, Firstborn, Inheritance)*

Christ	*Heb 1:2*
By promise	*Gal 3:29*
By faith	*Rom 4:13–14*
Through God	*Gal 4:7*
The recipient of:	
Kingdom	*James 2:5*
Salvation	*Heb 1:14*
Eternal life	*Titus 3:7*
Promise	*Heb 11:9*

HELL *(See also Eternity, Second Death, Sheol)*
Everlasting:

Fire	*Matt 25:41*
Punishment	*Matt 25:46*
Destruction	*2 Thess 1:9*

Residents of:

Devil	*Matt 25:41*
Fallen angels	*2 Pet 2:4*
Disobedient	*Rom 2:8–9*
Beast and false prophet	*Rev 19:20*

HERESY *(See also Apostasy)*

How to recognize	*2 John 9–11*
Avoiding fellowship with	*Gal 1:7–9*
Warning to teachers of	*Titus 3:10–11*

HERMON, MOUNT

East of Jordan	*Josh 12:1–5*

HEROD

The Great	*Luke 1:5*

Antipas:

Tetrarch of Galilee and Perea	*Luke 3:1*
Imprisoned John the Baptist	*Matt 14:1–12*
Had John beheaded	*Mark 6:22–28*
Pilate sent Jesus to	*Luke 23:7–11*

Agrippa I:

Killed James	*Acts 12:1–2*
Imprisoned Peter	*Acts 12:3–11*
Death of	*Acts 12:20–23*

Agrippa II:

Paul's defense before	*Acts 26:1–23*
Rejection of the gospel	*Acts 26:27–29*

HERODIAS

Wife of Herod's brother Philip	*Mark 6:17*
Planned death of John the Baptist	*Matt 14:1–10;*
	Mark 6:14–29

HEZEKIAH

Life of extended	*2 Kings 20:1–11*
Pride of	*2 Kings 20:12–19*
Death of	*2 Kings 20:21*
Carried out reforms in the temple	*2 Chron 29:3–36*
Prospered	*2 Chron 31:20–21*

HIRAM

Kings of Tyre	*2 Sam 5:11; 1 Kings 10:11*
Brass-worker to Solomon	*1 Kings 7:13*

HISTORY

Spiritual lessons from	*1 Cor 10:1–11; Heb 4:1–2*
Accuracy of the Word's	*2 Tim 3:16*

HOLINESS *(See also Consecration, Godliness, Sanctification)*

Christian's responsibility	*Eph 4:22–24; 1 Pet 1:15*
Call to	*Rom 12:1*
Comes through grace	*Titus 2 :11–12*
Possessed by Christ	*Luke 1:35; Acts 4:27*
Attained by the discipline of God	*Heb 12:10*

HOLY PLACE *(See Sanctuary, Tabernacle)*

HOLY SPIRIT *(See also Comforter, Fruit of the Spirit)*
Characteristics of:

Omniscience	*1 Cor 2:10*
Omnipresence	*Ps 139:7*
Teaches	*John 14:26*
Comforts	*Acts 9:31*
Can be grieved	*Eph 4:30*
Convicts men	*John 16:8–11*
Fills believers	*Acts 2:4*
Gives power to believers	*Acts 1:8*
Gives guidance	*Acts 16:6–10*

HOME *(See also Hospitality)*

Witnessing to people at	*Luke 8:39*
Prophet not honored there	*Mark 6:4*
Hospitality in	*Acts 16:15*
Church in	*Philem 1:1–2*
Sharing of	*John 19:27*

Figurative:

As human body	*2 Cor 5:6*
Where Holy Spirit lives	*John 14:23*
Eternal	*2 Cor 5:1*

HOMOSEXUALITY *(See also Sexual Conduct)*

Condemned	*Gen 19:1–11, 24; Lev 18:22; Rom 1:26–27*

HONESTY *(See also Lying, Sincerity, Truthfulness)*

Blessing of	*Isa 33:15–16*

| In all things | *Heb 13:18* |
| Pleases God | *Ps 15:1–2* |

HONOR *(See also Respect, Reverence)*

Should be given to:

Parents	*Exod 20:12; Eph 6:2*
God	*1 Tim 1:17*
Widows	*1 Tim 5:3*
Christ	*John 5:23*

Shown by:

Giving to God first	*Prov 3:9*
Accompanies wisdom	*Prov 3:13–16*
Follows humility	*Prov 15:33*

HOPE *(See also Anchor, Spiritual; Assurance; Confidence)*

Characteristics of:

Blessed	*Titus 2:13*
Sure	*Heb 6:19*
Good	*2 Thess 2:16*

Of the Christian towards:

God	*Ps 39:7*
Christ	*1 Cor 15:19*
Salvation	*Rom 5:1–5*

Inspires:

Purity	*1 John 3:3*
Courage	*Rom 5:4–5*
Joy	*Rom 12:12*
Assurance	*Heb 6:18–19*

HOREB, MOUNT

Name for Mount Sinai	*Exod 3:1; 17:6; 33:6; Deut 1:6; 4:10*
Law given there	*Deut 4:10–14*

HORSE

Symbolic of:

Stubbornness	*Ps 32:9*
Poor judgment	*Jer 8:6*
Trust	*Hos 14:3*

Uses:

In war	*Exod 14:9*
For travel	*Deut 17:16*
In idolatry	*2 Kings 23:11*

HOSEA

Called by the Lord	*Hos 1:1*
Married to unfaithful wife	*Hos 1:2–3*
Marriage illustrates Israel's unfaithfulness	*Hos 4–5*

HOSPITALITY *(See also Benevolence, Home)*

A Christian practice	*Rom 12:13*
A quality of a bishop	*1 Tim 3:2*
A test of discipleship	*Matt 25:35*
Should be done willingly	*1 Pet 4:9*

Shown by:

Washing of feet	*Luke 7:44*
Kissing	*Luke 7:45*
Providing food and housing	*Luke 11:5–8*

HUMILITY *(See also Meekness, Modesty, Pride)*

Of Christ	*Matt 11:29*
God teaches	*Deut 8:3*
Needed to receive grace	*James 4:6*
God is with those who have	*Isa 57:15*
Of a child	*Matt 18:4*

HUSBAND *(See also Bridegroom, Marriage, Wife)*

Sanctified by his wife	*1 Cor 7:16*
Head of his wife	*1 Cor 11:3*
Responsibility to wife:	
Be faithful	*Mal 2:14–15*
Instruct	*1 Cor 14:34–35*
Love	*Eph 5:25–33*
Live with	*Matt 19:3–9*
Provide for	*1 Tim 5:8*

HYMN *(See also Music, Song)*

Used for:	
Joyful expressions	*Matt 26:30*
Edification	*Eph 5:19; 1 Cor 14:15*
Worshiping God	*2 Chron 23:18*
Inspired by:	
Victories	*Judg 5:1–31*
Deliverance	*Exod 15:1–19*
Answered prayer	*1 Sam 2:1–10*
Joy	*Luke 1:46–56*

HYPOCRISY *(See also Honesty, Integrity)*

Ascribed to Pharisees and scribes	*Matt 23:13–15*

Pharisee's leaven is symbolic of	*Luke 12:1*

Description of:

Deceptive lives	*Ezek 33:31–32*
Unclean hearts	*Luke 11:39*
Blindness	*Matt 23:17–26*
Seeks self-acclaim	*Matt 6:2–5*

I

IDOLATRY *(See also Abomination, Baal)*

Results in:

Bondage	*Gal 4:8–9*
Degradation	*Rom 1:22–23*

Condemnation of:

Making images	*Exod 20:4; Lev 26:1*
Serving	*Exod 20:5; Ps 81:9*

IGNORANCE *(See also Knowledge, Wisdom)*

Sin because of	*Acts 3:17*
In former state	*Pet 1:14*
Of the Scriptures	*Matt 22:29*
Due to hardness of heart	*Eph 4:18*
From choice	*2 Pet 3:5*

IMMORALITY *(See also Lust, Morality, Sin)*

Condemned	*1 Cor 6:9*
No repentance for	*1 Cor 5:1*
Characterized by sexual perversion	*Rom 1:24–32*

IMMORTALITY *(See also Death, Eternity, Life)*

Through Jesus	John 3:15; 2 Tim 1:10
Given to those who are patient in well doing	Rom 2:7
Victory over death	1 Cor 15:53–54
Ascribed to God	1 Tim 1:17
Of the righteous	Matt 25:46
Gift of God	Rom 6:23
Promise of	1 John 2:25

IMPATIENCE *(See also Intolerance, Patience)*

Dealing with	Rom 5:3–4; Eph 4:1–3
Of Moses	Numbers 20:7–12
Of Martha at death of Lazarus	John 11:20–21
Of Jesus' mother at the wedding	John 2:3
Of Jesus' parents in the temple	Luke 2:48–49

INCARNATION *(See also Birth, Nativity)*

Purpose of	John 1:9–14
Spirits confess truth of	1 John 4:2
Foretold	John 7:42
Timing of	Gal 4:4

INCENSE *(See also Offering, Sacrifice, Temple)*

Offering of:

By priests	Lev 16:12–13
Exclusively for God	Exod 30:37–38

Symbolic of:

Prayer	Rev 5:8
Christ's intermediacy	Rev 8:3–4
Praise	Mal 1:11

INCEST *(See also Family, Sexual Conduct)*

Forbidden	*Lev 18:6–18*
Punishments for	*Lev 20:11–20; Deut 27:20–23*

INGRATITUDE *(See also Thankfulness)*

Remembered	*Deut 25:17–19*
Condemnation of	*2 Chron 32:25*

Causes of:

Opulence	*Deut 6:10–12*
Self-sufficiency	*Deut 8:12–18*
Pride	*Dan 5:18–20*
Negligence	*Luke 17:12–18*

INHERITANCE *(See also Birthright, Heir)*

By faith	*Gal 3:18–22*
Incorruptible	*1 Pet 1:4*
In Christ	*Eph 1:11–12*

Of the believers:

Eternal life	*Matt 19:29*
Blessings	*1 Pet 3:9*
Kingdom of God	*Matt 25:34*
Honor	*Prov 3:35*

INJUSTICE *(See also Justice, Law, Righteousness)*

Those who practice it shall perish	*Prov 11:7*
Command to avoid	*Lev 19:15*
The Lord avenges	*1 Thess 4:6*

INSANITY

Sent as judgment from God	*Deut 28:28*

Feigned by David   *1 Sam 21:13–15*
Jesus accused of   *Mark 3:21*

INSOMNIA *(See also Sleep)*

Of the rich   *Eccles 5:12*
Promise to claim regarding   *Prov 3:24*

INSPIRATION *(See also Revelation)*

Of Scripture   *2 Tim 3:16; Heb 1:1; 2 Pet 1:21*
By a voice   *Acts 8:29*
By a vision   *Ezek 11:24*
By a dream   *Dan 7:1*

INSTABILITY *(See also Change, Faithfulness, Steadfastness)*

In service   *Matt 6:24*
In faith   *James 1:7–8*
From disobedience   *Matt 7:26–27*

INSTRUCTION *(See also Teacher)*

By priests   *Lev 10:11*
By the Word   *2 Tim 3:16*
From nature   *Matt 6:25–30*
By prophets   *Heb 1:1*
By object lessons   *Jer 27:2–11; 28; Ezek 4:1–3*

INTEGRITY *(See also Character, Honesty, Sincerity)*

As protection   *Ps 25:21*
As guide   *Prov 11:3*
In trials   *Job 2:9*

INTERCESSION *(See also Mediator, Prayer, Substitution)*

Of Christ for believers	*Heb 7:25*
By the Holy Spirit for believers	*Rom 8:26–27*

INTOLERANCE *(See also Bigotry, Tolerance)*

Not to be a part of the Christian life	*Eph 4:1–3*

ISAAC *(See also Rebecca)*

Named by God	*Gen 17:19*
Born to Sarah in her old age	*Gen 17:15–16*
Descendants of are children of promise	*Rom 9:7–12*
Married to Rebecca	*Gen 24:63–67*

ISAIAH

Prophet during reigns of four kings	*Isa 1:1*
Foretold punishment of Jews for idolatry	*Isa 2:6–20*
Foretold the coming of Messiah	*Isa 9:1–7*
Prophesied judgments on other nations	*Isa 10:5–34*
Promised restoration of the Jews	*Isa 43:1–13*
Foretold conversion of the Gentiles	*Isa 45:5–25*

ISHMAEL

Son of Abraham	*Gen 16:11*
Promises concerning	*Gen 16:11–12; 17:20*
Sent away by Abraham	*Gen 21:6–21*

ISRAEL *(See also Jacob)*

New name of Jacob	*Gen 32:28*
Name given to descendants of	*Gen 43:32*

What God required of	*Deut 10:12–22*
Final conversion of	*Rom 11:26–27*
Administered by judges	*Judg 2:16–19*
Administered by kings:	
Saul	*1 Sam 8:22; 10:1; 11:15; 13:1*
David	*2 Sam 5:3–4*
Solomon	*1 Kings 1:38–39*

J

JACOB

Son of Isaac and brother of Esau	*Gen 25:24–26*
Cheated brother out of blessing	*Gen 27:1–29*
Father of twelve sons	*Gen 35:22*
Father of Joseph	*37:2*

JAEL

Israelite heroine	*Judg 4:17; 5:24*

JAIRUS

Jewish leader whose daughter was brought back to life	*Matt 9:18; Mark 5:22; Luke 8:41*

JAMES, SON OF ALPHAEUS

Christ appeared to after resurrection	*1 Cor 15:7*
Spoke on behalf of Gentile converts	*Acts 15:14–21*
Wrote epistle	*James 1:1*

JAMES, SON OF ZEBEDEE

An apostle	Matt 4:21–22
Fisherman and brother of John	Luke 5:10
Present at Transfiguration	Matt 17:1
Martyred	Acts 12:2

JAPHETH

Son of Noah	Gen 9:27

JASON

Persecuted at Thessalonica	Acts 17:5; Rom 16:21

JEALOUSY (See also Covetousness, Envy)

In man:

Makes him furious	Prov 6:34
Causes strife	1 Cor 3:3

Example of:

Joseph's brothers	Gen 37:4

JEHOAHAZ

Son of Jehu, king of Israel	2 Kings 10:35; 13:4
Evil king of Judah	2 Kings 23:31; 2 Chron 36:1

JEHOIACHIN

Defeated and taken captive	2 Chron 36:8–10

JEHOIADA

High priest killed Athaliah, restoring Jehoash	2 Kings 11:4
Repaired the temple	2 Kings 12:7
Abolished idolatry	2 Chron 23:16

JEHOIAKIM

Evil king of Judah taken captive   *2 Kings 23:34–24:1;*
                                            2 Chron 36:4–8; Dan 1:2

JEHORAM

Son of Jehoshaphat, king of Judah   *1 Kings 22:50*
(Joram) Son of Ahab, king of Israel   *2 Kings 1:17*

JEHOSHAPHAT

Good king of Judah   *1 Kings 15:24*

JEHU

Son of Hanani   *1 Kings 16:1; 23 Chron 19:2*
Son of Nimshi, king of Israel   *1 Kings 19:16; 2 Kings 9:1*

JEPHTHAH

Judge of israel   *Judg 11:1–34*

JEROBOAM *(See also Rehoboam)*

Rebelled against King solomon   *1 Kings 11:26*
Fled to Egypt to escape Solomon   *1 Kings 11:40*
First king of Israel after the revolt   *1 Kings 12:20*
Instituted idol worship   *1 Kings 12:28–29*

JEREMIAH

Priest and Prophet   *Jer 1:1*
Called by the Lord   *Jer 1:4–19*
Sent letter at prophecy to exiles   *Jer 29:1–32*
Persecuted for prophesying   *Jer 20:1–2*

JERICHO

Called City of Palm Trees	*Deut 34:3*
Besieged by Joshua seven days	*Josh 6:1–16*
Walls fell at trumpet blast and shouts	*Josh 6:20*
Where Jesus healed blind man	*Matt 20:29–34*

JERUSALEM *(See also Zion)*

Called City of the Great King	*Ps 48:2*
Capital of David's kingdom	*1 Kings 15:4*
Feasts of Jews held at	*Ezek 36:38*
Prayer center of Israelites	*1 Kings 8:37–39*
Ark brought to	*2 Sam 6:12–19*
Temple built in	*2 Chron 3:1*
Captured by king of Babylon	*2 Chron 36:17–20*
Rebuilt walls of	*Neh 2:20; 7:1*
Gospel first preached in	*Luke 24:47*

JESSE

David's father	*Ruth 4:17–22*
His posterity	*1 Chron 2:13*

JESUS CHRIST *(See also Christ)*

Pre-existence	*John 8:58*
Deity	*Rom 9:5; Col 2:9*
Wisdom	*1 Cor 1:30; Col 2:3*
Subordinate to Father	*John 5:19; 14:28*
Creator	*John 1:2–3; Col 1:15–16*
Incarnation	*Matt 1:18–21; John 1:1–18*
Teaching	*Matt 5–7, 13*
Miracles	*Matt 14:13–21; 23–29; Luke 7:13–15*

Death	*Matt 27:31–54; John 19:17–30*
Resurrection	*John 20:11–18*
Ascension	*Acts 1:9–11*
As way of salvation	*John 14:6; Acts 4:12*
Second Adam	*Rom 5:12–21; 1 Cor 15:22–45*
Image of God	*Col 1:15*
Author of faith and grace	*Heb 12:12; 2 Cor 12:9*
Redeemer	*1 Cor 1:30; Gal 3:13; Col 1:14*
And the Law	*Matt 5:17–19; Rom 10:14*
Sinlessness	*2 Cor 5:21*
Significance of his death	*Col 2:14–15*
Faith in him	*Rom 3:26; 10:13; John 1:12; John 3:23*
Union with him	*Gal 2:16–20; Col 2:11–13*
Return	*John 14:3; 1 Thess 4:16; 5:1–11*
Judge	*2 Cor 5:10; 2 Tim 2:4*
Lord	*Phil 2:9–11*
Sustainer of Christians	*Jude 24*
High priest for Christians	*Heb 7:15–10:20*

JETHRO

Moses' father-in-law	*Exod 18:12*

JEWELRY

Brought as an offering	*Exod 35:22*
Used by kings as symbol of authority	*Esther 8:1–2*

JOAB

Nephew of David	*2 Sam 8:16*
Killed Abner	*2 Sam 3:23*
Killed Absolom	*2 Sam 18:14*

Joined Adonijah's usurpation   *1 Kings 1:7*

JOASH

(Jehoash) King of Israel   *2 Kings 13:10*
King of Judah   *2 Kings 11:4; 2 Chron 23:1–24:23*

JOB

Afflicted by Satan   *Job 1:6–2:6*
Patience of in trial   *Job 1:21*
Questioned his plight   *Job 10:1–7*
Tried to vindicate himself   *Job 23:10–12; 27:1–6*
Answered by God   *Job 38:1–41:34*

JOEL

Foretold judgments   *Joel 2:1–11*
Foretold giving of God's Spirit   *Joel 2:28–29*

JOHN, APOSTLE

With Jesus in Gethsemane   *Mark 14:33*
Called pillar of the church   *Gal 2:9*
Took care of Jesus' mother   *John 19:26*
Called the disciple whom Jesus loved   *John 13:23*
Wrote of his revelation on Patmos   *Rev 1:9–11*

JOHN THE BAPTIST *(See also Elisabeth)*

Birth foretold by angel   *Luke 1:11–13*
Preached the coming of Jesus   *Mark 1:7*
Witnessed that Jesus was deity   *John 1:29–34*
Baptized Jesus   *Mark 1:9–10*
Preached repentance and baptism   *Matt 3:6*

Imprisoned and beheaded by Herod   *Matt 14:1–12*

JONAH
Prophet of God   *Jon 1:1*
Disobeyed God   *Jon 1:2–3*
Swallowed by large fish   *Jon 1:17*
Delivered from fish   *Jon 2:10*
Obeyed God   *Jon 3:1–5*

JONATHAN
Son of Saul   *1 Sam 13:2*
His love for David   *1 Sam 18:1*
Killed by Philistines   *1 Sam 31:2*

JOPPA
Tabitha raised from dead there   *Acts 9:36*
Peter lived there   *Acts 10:5; 11:5*

JORDAN, RIVER
Miraculously separated for crossing   *Josh 3:14–16*
Naaman washed in to heal leprosy   *2 Kings 5:10–14*
Jesus baptized in   *Matt 3:13*

JOSEPH
Favorite son of Jacob   *Gen 37:3*
Sold to Egypt by brothers   *Gen 37:27*
Interpreted dreams   *Gen 40:5–23; 41:1–37*
Named to prepare for famine   *Gen 41:39–40, 48–49*
Forgave and helped his brothers   *Gen 45:1–15*

JOSHUA

Pleaded with Israelites to go to Canaan	Num 14:5–9
Succeeded Moses	Num 27:18–23
Led people to Canaan	Josh 1–4
Besieged and took Jericho	Josh 6
Challenged Israelites to serve God	Josh 24:14–15

JOSIAH

King of Judah	2 Kings 22:1–23:9

JOTHAM

King of Judah	2 Kings 15:32

JOY *(See also Happiness, Victory)*

Of the Lord	Neh 8:10

Occasions for:

In believing	Isa 12:3; Rom 15:13
In the Holy Spirit	Rom 14:17
Because of what God has done	Ps 92:4
When a sinner repents	Luke 15:10
In trials	James 1:2

JUBILEE, YEAR OF

Description	Lev 25:10, 28; 27:17
Symbolic	Isa 61:2; Luke 4:19

JUDAH *(See also Israel)*

One of tribes of Israel	Gen 49:8–12, 28
Led in occupation of Canaan	Judg 1:1–2
David, king of	2 Sam 5:5

Remained loyal to David in revolts   *2 Sam 20:1–2*

JUDAS *(See also Apostle)*
Apostle (also called Jude or Thaddeus)   *Luke 6:16*

JUDAS ISCARIOT
Disciple who betrayed Jesus   *Matt 10:4; 26:14, 47*

JUDGES OF ISRAEL
Provided by God   *Judg 2:16, 18*
People would not listen to   *Judg 2:17*
Instances of corrupt:
Eli's sons   *1 Sam 2:12*
Samuel's sons   *1 Sam 8:1–3*

JUDGMENT *(See also Condemnation, Punishment)*
Of God:
Will come to all   *Acts 17:31; 1 Cor 4:5*
Administered by Christ   *2 Cor 5:10*
Description of   *Matt 25:31–46; 1 Thess 1:5–10*
Comes after death   *Heb 9:27*

JUSTICE *(See also Courts, Mercy, Righteousness)*
Of God   *Ps 75:1–10; Ezek 18:25*
Lack of   *Isa 59:14; Mic 7:3; John 7:24*
Need for   *Prov 24:23; Isa 1:17; Zech 8:16*
God loves   *Ps 37:28*

JUSTIFICATION *(See Atonement, Justice,*
Righteousness)

Not by the Law	*Rom 3:20; Gal 3:11*
By faith	*Acts 13:39; Rom 1:17*
By works	*James 2:14–26*

K

KADESH BARNEA

Where Israelites murmured against Moses and Aaron	*Num 13:26; 14:1–45*

KETURAH

Abraham's second wife	*Gen 25:1–4*

KEY

Symbol of authority	*Matt 16:19; Rev 1:18*
Of David	*Rev 3:7*

KIDRON

Brook crossed by David	*2 Sam 15:23*
Idols destroyed there	*1 Kings 15:13; 2 Kings 23:6*
Frequented by Jesus	*John 18:1*

KINDNESS *(See also Benevolence, Love, Tolerance)*

Of the Lord	*1 Pet 2:3*
In speech	*Prov 31:26*
In ministry	*2 Cor 6:6*
Among believers	*Eph 4:32; Col 3:12*

To those in need   *1 John 3:17*
To all   *Gal 6:10*

KING *(See also Authority)*

Israelites asked for a   *1 Sam 8:4–5*
Israelites rejected God as   *1 Sam 8:7; 10:19*
Samuel warns about life under a   *1 Sam 8:10–18*
Saul was first   *1 Sam 9:27–10:1*
Chosen by divine appointment   *1 Sam 16:1–13*
God as   *Ps 24:7; 1 Tim 1:17*

KINGDOM *(See also Heaven, Zion)*

Of God   *1 Chron 29:11; Ps 22:28*
Of Christ   *Matt 16:28; 2 Pet 1:11*
Of heaven   *Matt 7:21; 25:1*
Of the world   *Rev 11:15*

KIRIATH (KIRJATH) JEARIM

Where Ark rested for 20 years   *1 Sam 7:2*

KISSING

As greeting in early church   *Rom 16:16; 1 Cor 16:20*

KNEELING *(See also Humility, Prayer)*

In prayer   *2 Chron 6:13*
Stephen, during his stoning   *Acts 7:59–60*
Before God   *Eph 3:14*
Ezra, in shame for his people   *Neh 9:5–6*

KNOWLEDGE *(See also Learning, Philosophy, Wisdom)*

Of God	*Prov 3:20*
Of Christ	*Phil 3:8*
Of salvation	*Luke 1:77*
Gift of	*1 Cor 12:8*
Is pleasant	*Prov 2:10*
More valuable than gold	*Prov 8:10*

L

LABAN

Gave Jacob his two daughters	*Gen 29:1–30*
Envied and oppressed Jacob	*Gen 30:27; 31:1*
Covenant with Jacob	*Gen 31:43–55*

LAMB *(See also Offering)*

Of God	*John 1:29*
As an offering	*Exod 29:38*
Figurative:	
Of Christ	*Rev 5:12*
Of believers	*John 21:15*

LAMECH

Father of Noah	*Gen 5:25, 29*

LAMENESS *(See also Handicapped, Health)*

Healed	*Matt 11:5; Luke 7:22; Acts 3:2–8*

LAMP (See also Light)
God's Word is a	Ps 119:105
A father's commandment is a	Prov 6:23

Figurative of:
The eye	Luke 11:34
The wicked	Prov 13:9

LANGUAGE (See also Mouth, Speech)
Gift of, by Holy Spirit	Acts 2:4
One, on earth	Gen 11:1
More than one, after Babel	Gen 11:7–9

LAODICEA
Paul's letter to	Col 2:1; 4:16
Christ's message to the church there	Rev 3:14–22

LAUGHTER
A time for	Eccles 3:4
Of Israel	Ps 126:2

LAW (See also Courts, Justice, Ten Commandments)
Of the Lord	Ps 19:7
Given through Moses	Exod 20
All of it must be obeyed	Gal 3:10
No one justified by it	Rom 3:20
Saved from curse of	Gal 3:13
Christ is end of the	Rom 10:4

LAZARUS
Parable of the beggar	Luke 16:19–31

Brother of Mary and Martha:

Illness of   *John 11:1–4*

Death of   *John 11:14*

Raised from the dead   *John 11:38–44*

LEADERSHIP *(See also Authority, Head, Minister)*

By those who don't know the way   *Matt 15:13–14*

Of God   *Ps 23:2–3; 37:23; Exod 20:2*

Instances of:

Moses   *Exod 6:13; 14:13–14, 21*

Deborah   *Judg 4:4–15*

LEAH

Wife of Jacob   *Gen 29:16, 31; 30:17; 31:4; 33:2*

LEARNING *(See also Knowledge, Wisdom)*

Need to increase in   *Prov 1:5*

With God's help   *Dan 1:17*

Testing authority in   *John 7:17*

LEBANON

Cedars from, used to build Temple   *1 Kings 5:6–18*

LEVI

Son of Jacob   *Gen 29:34*

Avenged his sister Dinah's defilement   *Gen 34:1–31*

LIBERALITY *(See also Generosity)*

Object of:

Poor   *Deut 15:11*

All men	*Gal 6:10*
Purpose of:	
Demonstrating one's faith	*James 2:14–16*
Securing true riches	*1 Tim 6:17–19*
Blessings of:	
Honored by Christ	*Matt 25:40*
Rewarded	*Prov 3:9–10*

LIBERTY

Christians called to	*Gal 5:13*
Christian law of	*James 1:25*
Not causing offense	*Rom 14:13–23*
Walk in	*Ps 119:44–45*
Proclaimed by Jesus	*Luke 4:16–21; John 8:31–36*

LIFE *(See also Immortality)*
Natural:

Brevity of	*Ps 90:9–10*
Put Kingdom of God first in	*Matt 6:25–33*
Given up for Christ	*Matt 10:39*
Spiritual:	
Source of	*John 14:6*
Described	*John 3:3–8*
Evidence of	*1 John 3:14*
Eternal	*John 3:15*

LIGHT *(See also Darkness, Lamp)*
Descriptive of:

God	*1 John 1:5*
Jesus Christ	*John 8:12*

Christians	*Matt 5:14*
God's Word	*Ps 119:105*
Christian life	*1 John 1:7; 2:9–10*

LION
King of animals	*Prov 30:30*
Used figuratively of:	
Tribe of Judah	*Gen 49:9*
Jesus Christ	*Rev 5:5*
Devil	*1 Pet 5:8*
Antichrist	*Rev 13:2*

LOCUSTS *(See also Pestilence)*
| Used as a judgment | *Exod 10:12–19; Deut 28:38, 42* |
| Used for food | *Matt 3:4* |

LOIS
| Grandmother of Timothy | *2 Tim 1:5* |

LONELINESS *(See also Comfort)*
Instances of:	
Joseph	*Gen 43:30*
Jeremiah	*Jer 15:17*
Jesus	*Matt 26:36–45*
Paul	*2 Tim 4:16*

LONGEVITY *(See also Old Age, Youth)*
Allotted years	*Ps 90:10*
Increased by:	
Fearing the Lord	*Prov 9:10–11; 10:27*

Wisdom	*Prov 3:13, 16*
Honoring parents	*Eph 6:1–3*

LONG-SUFFERING *(See also Patience, Tolerance)*

Descriptive of God's character	*2 Pet 3:9*
Exemplified by the prophets	*James 5:10*
Produced by the Spirit	*Gal 5:22*
To characterize believers	*Eph 4:1–2*
Needed by pastors	*2 Tim 4:1–2*

LORD

Title applied to:

God	*Gen 3:8–9, 14; Lev 19:2*
Jesus Christ	*Luke 6:46; Acts 1:21; Rev 22:20*
Confessing that Jesus is	*Rom 10:9; Phil 2:11*

LORD'S DAY *(See also Sabbath)*

First day of week	*John 20:1, 19*
Breaking bread on	*Acts 20:7*
The Lord spoke to John on	*Rev 1:10*

LORD'S PRAYER *(See also Prayer)*

Taught to disciples	*Matt 6:9–13; Luke 11:1–4*
Believers using as example	*Matt 6:9*

LORD'S SUPPER *(See also Communion, Eucharist)*

Instituted by Christ	*Matt 26:26–29*
Observed by early church	*Acts 2:42, 46*
Instructions concerning	*1 Cor 11:23–34*
Commemorative of Christ's death	*Luke 22:19–20*

LOT
Abraham's nephew	*Gen 13:10*
Saved from Sodom	*Gen 19:1–26*

LOVE *(See also Affection, Altruism, Kindness)*
Towards God commanded	*Deut 6:5*
Towards neighbor commanded	*Matt 22:39*
Exemplified by Christ	*John 15:13*
To be shown among believers	*John 15:12*
Obedience as proof of	*John 14:15*
Defined	*1 Cor 13:4–7*
Importance of	*1 Cor 13:1–3, 8–13*
Of the world condemned	*1 John 2:15–17*

LOYALTY *(See also Character, Faithfulness)*
Urged as fitting	*Prov 24:21; Rom 13:1–2; Titus 3:1*
Displayed by disciples	*John 6:67–69*
Promised to believers by Jesus	*Heb 13:5*
Part of God's character	*Deut 7:9*

LUCIFER *(See also Satan)*
A name of Satan	*Isa 14:12–14*

LUKE
Doctor and companion to Paul	*Col 4:14; 2 Tim 4:11*

LUST *(See also Adultery, Fornication, Immorality)*
Originating in man's heart	*Matt 15:19*
Christ provided an escape from	*2 Pet 1:4*
Leads to sin	*James 1:14–15*

Turning away from   *2 Tim 2:22*
Part of unbeliever's's life   *Eph 2:3*

LYDIA

First convert in Philippi   *Acts 16:13–15*

LYING *(See also Accusation, False; Deceit; Dishonesty)*

Counted as an abomination   *Prov 6:16–19*
Prayer for deliverance from   *Ps 120:2*
Originating with the devil   *John 8:44*
Denial that Jesus is the Christ   *1 John 2:21–23*
Associated with disobedience   *1 John 2:4*
The wicked take pleasure in   *Ps 62:4*

LYSTRA

Where Paul healed cripple, was worshiped,
   then stoned   *Acts 14:8–20*

M

MACEDONIA

Paul's mission there   *Acts 16:9*
Generosity of   *2 Cor 8:1–5*

MAGIC *(See also Astrology, Occult, Witchcraft)*

Condemned by law   *Lev 20:27*
Those practicing judged   *Rev 21:8*
Failed to drive out demon   *Acts 19:13–16*
Those who had practiced   *Acts 19:19*

MAGICIAN *(See also Magic)*

Condemned by law	*Lev 20:27*
Helpless in plagues	*Exod 8:18*
Believed and was baptized	*Acts 8:13, 18–24*

MAJESTY *(See also Glory, King, Presence of God)*

Of God:

Glory of	*Isa 2:19*
Clothed with	*Ps 93:1*

Of Christ:

Foretold	*Mic 5:2–4*
Witnessed	*2 Pet 1:16–17*

MALACHI

Prophet of God	*Mal 1:1*
Described sins of the priests	*Mal 1:6–14*
Described sins of the people	*Mal 3:6–9, 13–15*
Foretold coming of Elijah and Christ	*Mal 3:1–3; 4:5–6*

MALCHUS

High priest's servant whose ear was cut off	*John 18:10*

MALICE *(See also Evil, Sin)*

Comes from perverted heart	*Prov 6:14, 18–19*
Christians to rid themselves of	*1 Cor 5:7–8; Eph 4:31*

MAMMON

Worship of	*Matt 6:24 (KJV)*

MAN *(See also Woman)*

Created for God's glory	*Isa 43:7*
Created by God	*Gen 1:26–27*
Made in God's image	*Gen 9:6*
Wonderfully made	*Ps 139:13–16*
Sin entered through disobedience	*Gen 3:1–7*
By one, sin came into the world	*Rom 5:12*
Continues eternally	*Matt 25:46*
Parity with others before God	*Prov 22:2*

MANASSEH

Evil king of Judah	*2 Kings 21:1–18*

Son of Joseph:

Firstborn	*Gen 41:51*
His blessing and inheritance	*Gen 48:1–20*

MANNA *(See also Bread)*

Supplied by God	*Exod 16:4, 15; John 6:31–32*
Despised by people	*Num 11:4–6*

MARAH

Where bitter water was made sweet	*Exod 15:23*

MARK (JOHN MARK)

Cousin of Barnabas	*Col 4:10*
Accompanied Paul and Barnabas	*Acts 13:5*
Left Paul and Barnabas	*Acts 13:13*
Paul and Barnabas argue over	*Acts 15:37–40*
Comforted Paul in prison	*Col 4:10*

MARRIAGE *(See also Adultery, Bride, Polygamy)*

Instituted by God	Gen 2:18–24
Honorable for all	Heb 13:4
Intimate and permanent bond	Matt 19:5–6
Dissolved by death	Rom 7:2–3
Means of preventing immorality	1 Cor 7:2–4

Figurative of:

God's union with Israel	Isa 54:5
Christ's union with his church	Eph 5:23–32

MARTHA

Sister of Mary	Luke 10:38
Sister of Lazarus	John 11:1, 17–27

MARTYRDOM

Not to be feared	Matt 10:28
To be accepted if necessary	Acts 21:13

Examples of:

John the Baptist	Mark 6:18–29
Stephen	Acts 7:58–60
Heroes of faith	Heb 11:35–37

MARY

Mother of Jesus, wife of Joseph	Matt 1:1–16
Observed Jesus' first miracle	John 2:1–10
Was present at crucifixion	John 19:25–26
Cared for by the disciple	John 19:27

MARY MAGDALENE

Delivered of demons by Jesus	Luke 8:2

Helped Jesus and disciples   *Luke 1:1–3*
Was present at crucifixion   *John 19:25*
Was first to see Jesus after resurrection   *John 20:14–18*

MATTHEW *(See also Apostle)*

Apostle (also called Levi)   *Matt 9:9*
Sent out   *Matt 10:3; Acts 1:13*

MEDIATOR *(See also Jesus Christ)*

Christ as:
Between God and man   *1 Tim 2:5*
Of a new covenant   *Heb 8:6; 9:15*
A continuing high priest   *Heb 7:24*
Intercessor   *1 John 2:1*

MEDICINE *(See also Health, Physician, Sickness)*

Cheerful heart as   *Prov 17:22*
Insufficient remedy   *Isa 1:6*
Used by Good Samaritan   *Luke 10:34*

MEDITATION *(See also Prayer)*

On God's Word   *Ps 119:97–99*
On God's law   *Ps 1:2*
On God's work   *Ps 77:12*
For understanding   *Ps 49:3*

MEEKNESS *(See also Humility, Submission)*

Serving in spirit of   *James 3:13*
Among the fruits of the spirit   *Gal 5:22–23*
Characteristic of Christ   *Matt 11:29; 27:12–14*

MELCHIZEDEK

King of Salem who blessed Abraham   *Gen 14:18*
His priesthood   *Ps 110:4; Heb 5:6, 10; 6:20; 7:1*

MEPHIBOSHETH

Lame son of Jonathan   *2 Sam 4:4*
Cherished and spared by David   *2 Sam 9:1; 21:7*

MERCY *(See also Forgiveness, Grace)*

Characteristic of God   *Lam 3:22–23*
To characterize believers   *Matt 5:7; Luke 6:36*
God showed in salvation   *Titus 3:4–5*
Underlies hope of eternal life   *Jude 21*

MESHACH *(See also Shadrach, Abednego)*

His faith, suffering, and deliverance with Shadrach and
    Abednego   *Dan 1:1–7; 3:1–30*

MESSIAH *(See also Jesus Christ, Anointed One)*

Promised as seed of Abraham   *Gal 3:16*
Descended from tribe of Judah   *Gen 49:10*
A king of David's lineage   *Jer 23:5; Luke 1:32–33*
Described as Son of Man   *Dan 7:13–14; Mark 8:38*
Preached the Good News   *Isa 61:1–3; Luke 4:17–19*
Jesus confirmed that he was   *John 13:19*
Paul preached that Jesus was   *Acts 17:2–3*

METHUSELAH

Oldest man who lived   *Gen 5:27*

MICAH

Prophet of God	*Mic 1:1*
Told of God's anger	*Mic 1:2–16*
Described the sin of Israel, Judah	*Mic 2:1–2, 3:1–12*
Told of Messiah's coming	*Mic 5:2–4*

MICHAEL

Archangel	*Jude 9; Rev 12:7*

MICHAL

David's wife	*1 Sam 18:20*
Mocks his religious dancing, rebuked	*2 Sam 6:16, 20*

MIDIAN

Where Moses fled after killing Egyptian	*Exod 1:11–22*

MILK *(See also Food)*
Figurative:

Spiritual food	*1 Pet 2:2*
Food for new believers	*1 Cor 3:2*
Food for immature believers	*Heb 5:11–14*

MILLENNIUM

Described	*Rev 20:1–6*

MIND *(See also Heart, Soul, Will)*

Loving God with	*Matt 22:37*
Of Christ in believers	*Phil 2:5; 1 Cor 2:16*
Renewal of in believers	*Rom 12:2*
Of unregenerate is hostile	*Col 1:21*

Unity of	Phil 2:1–2
Spirit-controlled brings peace	Rom 8:6
Humble	1 Pet 3:8

MINISTER *(See also Pastor, Servant)*

Example of Christ	Mark 10:45

Should be:

Able to teach	1 Tim 3:2
Courageous	Acts 20:22–24
Diligent	1 Cor 15:10
Faithful	1 Cor 4:2
Meek	Gal 6:1
Prayerful	Acts 6:4
Filled with Holy Spirit	Acts 1:8
An example in talk and behavior	1 Tim 4:12

MINISTRY *(See also Minister, Servant)*

Of angels	Ps 103:20
As servanthood	Matt 20:22–27
Of God's messengers	1 Cor 3:5

Examples of:

Preaching the gospel	1 Cor 1:17
Building up the church	John 21:15–17; Eph 4:12
Praying for others	Col 1:9
Teaching	2 Tim 2:2
Comforting the distressed	2 Cor 1:4–6

MIRACLE *(See also Sign)*

To reveal God's glory	John 11:40
To reveal Christ's glory	John 2:11

| Recorded to produce faith | *John 20:30–31* |

Attributed to:

God's power	*Acts 15:12*
Christ's power	*John 2:11*
Spirit's power	*Matt 12:28*

MIRIAM

Sister of Moses and Aaron	*Exod 15:20*
Song of	*Exod 15:20–21*
Murmured against Moses	*Num 12:1–2; 10, 15*

MISSION *(See also Evangelism)*

Of Christ:

To do God's will	*John 6:38*
To save the lost	*Luke 19:10*
To reveal God	*Heb 1:1–3*
To fulfil the law	*Matt 5:17*
To give his life	*Mark 10:45*

Of Christians:

| To make disciples | *Matt 28:16–20* |

MISSIONARY

Commission of	*Mark 16:15; 28:19*
Witness of	*1 Chron 16:23–24*
Message of	*Matt 24:14; Luke 24:47–48*

MIZPAH

| Jacob and Laban met there | *Gen 31:49* |
| Where Israel sacrificed, fasted and defeated Philistines | *1 Sam 7:5–11* |

137

MOAB

Son of Lot and his daughter   *Gen 19:36–37*
His descendants and territory   *Deut 2:9, 18; 34:5*

MOCKING

Objects of:
God   *2 Kings 19:4; Gal 6:7*
Christ   *Luke 23:11, 36; Matt 27:29*
Believers   *Heb 11:36*

MODESTY *(See also Humility, Pride)*

Encouraged in dress   *1 Tim 2:9; 1 Pet 3:3–4*

MOLECH

God to whom Canaanites sacrificed
    their children   *Lev 18:21; 2 Kings 23:10*

MONEY *(See also Commerce, Finances, Riches)*

Not to be loaned for interest   *Lev 25:37; Deut 23:19*
Love of, a root of evil   *1 Tim 6:10*
Given as an offering   *Deut 14:22–29*
Associated with greed   *2 King 5:19–27*
Used to pay taxes   *Matt 17:24–27; 22:17–21*
Used to repair temple   *2 Kings 12:13–14*

MORALITY/MORALS *(See also Behavior, Conduct)*

Ruined by bad company   *1 Cor 15:33*
Required by God's Law   *Deut 11:1*
Taught by Jesus   *Matt 5:17–48; 6:22–24; 7:7–12*
Preached by prophets   *Isa 1:17*

MORDECAI

Revealed plot against Ahasuerus	*Esther 2:21–23*
Plot against him thwarted by Esther	*Esther 3:1–7:10*

MORTALITY *(See also Death, Immortality)*

Consequence of sin	*Rom 5:12*
Death a common experience	*Heb 9:27*
End of earthly life	*Eccles 9:10*
All to be raised from death	*Acts 24:15*
A return to dust	*Gen 3:19*

MOSES *(See also Commandment, Exodus, Law)*

Descendant of Levi	*Exod 2:1*
Instructed in Egyptian wisdom	*Acts 7:22*
Refused Egyptian sonship	*Heb 11:24–27*
Called by God	*Exod 3:1–10*
Conflict with Pharaoh	*Exod 7–12*
Commanded to institute the Passover	*Exod 12:1–29*
Received the Law	*Exod 20–23*
Sent spies to Canaan	*Num 13:1–33*
Sinned in anger	*Num 20:1–33*
Commissioned Joshua	*Num 27:12–23*
Died in full strength at 120	*Deut 34:5–7*

MOTHERHOOD *(See also Fatherhood)*

Object of prayer	*Gen 25:21*
Makes joyful	*Ps 113:9*
Painful yet joyful	*John 16:21*

MOTIVE (See also Desire)

Ascribed to God	Ps 106:8; Ezek 36:21–22, 32
Right, required	Matt 6:1–18
Sinful, illustrated by Cain	1 John 3:12

MOUNTAIN

Significant Old Testament events on:

Ark's resting place	Gen 8:4
Giving of the Law	Exod 19:2
Combat with Baal priests	1 Kings 18:19–40

In Christ's life, place of:

Temptation	Matt 4:8
Sermon	Matt 5:1
Prayer	Matt 14:23
Transfiguration	Matt 17:1
Ascension	Luke 24:50

MOURNING (See also Bereavement, Sorrow)

Transformed into joy and gladness	Isa 51:11; 61:3

Caused by:

Death	Gen 23:2
Disobedience	Ezra 9:3–7
Desolation	Joel 1:8–10
Depravity	Prov 5:11

MOUTH (See also Conversation, Speech, Tongue)

Make all words acceptable	Ps 19:14
Guard carefully	Ps 39:1; 141:3
May the talk of be helpful	Eph 4:29
Keep foul language from	Col 3:8

MURDER *(See also Death, Hatred)*

An act of the sinful nature	*Matt 15:19*
Results from hatred	*Matt 5:21–22*
Guilt determined by witnesses	*Num 35:30*

MUSIC *(See also Hymn, Musical Instrument, Singing)*

Used in:

Entertainment	*Isa 5:12*
Weddings	*Jer 7:34*
Funerals	*Matt 9:23, 23*
Victory celebrations	*Exod 15:20–21*
Praising God	*Heb 2:12; Rev 14:2–3*
Fellowship	*Eph 5:19; Col 3:16*

MUSICAL INSTRUMENTS *(See also Harp, Music, Trumpet)*

List of:

Cymbals	*Ps 150:5; 1 Cor 13:1*
Flute, harp, lyre	*Ps 150:3; Isa 5:12; Dan 3:5, 7, 10*
Strings	*Ps 150:4*
Tambourine	*2 Sam 6:5; Ps 150:4; Isa 5:12*
Trumpets	*Ps 150:3; Rev 18:22*

MYSTERY *(See also Revelation, Secret)*

Christ's incarnation	*1 Tim 3:16*
Nature of Christ	*Col 2:2*
The indwelling Christ	*Col 1:26–27*
Communion of all Christians	*Eph 3:4–9*
Hardening of Israel's heart	*Rom 11:25*
Resurrection	*1 Cor 15:51–52*

N

NAHUM

Prophet of God	*Nah 1:1*
Described God's greatness and wrath	*Nah 1:1–14*
Predicted fall of Nineveh	*Nah 2:1–13*
Told reasons for its fall	*Nah 3:1–19*

NAME

Value of a good	*Prov 22:1*
Of believers:	
Will receive new	*Isa 62:2; Rev 3:12*
Written in heaven	*Luke 10:20*
Known by Christ	*John 10:3*
Christ's exalted	*Phil 2:9–10*

NAMES FOR GOD *(See also God, Jesus, Holy Spirit)*

Father	*John 12:49*
Most High	*Ps 83:18*
King of kings and Lord of lords	*1 Tim 6:15*
Judge	*Judg 11:27*
Lord	*Ps 16:2*

NAOMI

Ruth's mother-in-law	*Ruth 1:1–22*

NAPHTALI

Son of Jacob	*Gen 30:8*
Tribe of Israel	*Judg 1:33*

NATHAN
Prophesied to David	*2 Sam 7:1–17*
Anointed Solomon king	*1 Kings 1:34*

NATHANAEL
Called by Jesus	*John 1:44–50*

NATION *(See also Kingdom, Patriotism)*
Believers constitute a	*1 Pet 2:9–10*
Abraham father of many	*Gen 17:4–5*
Exalted by righteousness	*Prov 14:34*
Israel set apart	*Exod 19:5–6*
All organically connected	*Acts 17:26*
Gospel preached to every	*Matt 24:14; Rev 14:6*
Believers from every	*Rev 15:9*

NATIVITY *(See also Incarnation)*
Of Jesus	*Matt 1:18–25; Luke 2:1–7*

NAZARETH
Boyhood home of Jesus	*Matt 2:23; Luke 2:39–40*
Obscure town	*John 1:46*
Residents rejected Jesus	*Luke 4:16–30*

NAZIRITE
By birth	*Judg 13:5, 7*
By vow	*Num 6:2*
Requirements of	*Num 6:2–8*
Examples of:	
Samson	*Judg 16:17*

Samuel   *1 Sam 1:11*

NEBUCHADNEZZAR *(See also Babylon)*
Takes Jerusalem, carries captives to Babylon   *Dan 1:1–4*
Builder of Babylon   *Dan 4:30*
Instrument of God's judgment   *Jer 27:8*
Touched with insanity   *Dan 4:28–37*
Ruler of first of four great kingdoms   *Dan 2:30–40*

NEHEMIAH *(See also Ezra)*
Leader in the postexilic community   *Ezra 2:2*
Son of Hachaliah   *Neh 1:1*
Cupbearer to Artaxerxes I   *Neh 1:11*
Allowed to rebuild Jerusalem   *Neh 2:1–8*
Effects reform among Jews   *Neh 5:1–19*
Supports Ezra in restoration of worship   *Neh 8–10*

NEIGHBOR *(See also Friendship, Love)*
Love towards   *Rom 13:9–10*
Speak truth to   *Eph 4:25*
Urged to be   *Luke 10:29–37*
Coveting of possessions forbidden   *Exod 20:17*

NERVOUSNESS *(See Anxiety, Care, Impatience)*

NICODEMUS
Went to Jesus at night   *John 3:1–21*
Assisted at Christ's burial   *John 19:39*

NIGHT *(See also Darkness, Day)*

Named by God	*Gen 1:5*
Jesus prays through	*Luke 6:12*
None in heaven	*Rev 21:25; 22:5*
Figurative of ignorance and unbelief	*Rom 13:12; 1 Thess 5:5*

NINEVEH

Jonah's mission to	*Jonah 1:1; 3:2*
Spared by God after repentance	*John 3:5–10*

NOAH *(See also Ark, Rainbow)*

Son of Lamech	*Gen 5:28–29*
Father of Shem, Ham, and Japheth	*Gen 5:32*
Righteous man	*Gen 6:8–9*
Instructed to build ark	*Gen 6:14–16*
Saved from flood waters	*Gen 8:1–17*
Covenant established with	*Gen 9:1–19*
Died when 950	*Gen 9:29*

O

OATH *(See also Curse, Swearing)*

God's confirmation of	*Gen 26:3*
Taking of	*Neh 5:12*
Despising of	*Ezek 16:59*
False	*Zech 8:17*
Not taking of	*James 5:12*

OBADIAH

Prophet to Edom	*Obad 1:1*
Met Elijah	*1 Kings 18:7*
Hid 100 prophets	*1 Kings 18:4, 13*

OBEDIENCE *(See also Disobedience, Submission)*

To the Covenant	*Exod 24:7*
To God	*1 Sam 15:22*
To Christ	*2 Cor 10:5*
To the gospel	*2 Thess 1:8; 1 Pet 4:17*
To the faith	*Acts 6:7*
To parents	*Col 3:20*
To husbands	*Titus 2:5*

OBLIGATION *(See also Duty, Responsibility)*

To God	*Rom 14:12*
To believer	*John 8:24*
To other Christians	*1 John 3:16*
To live righteously	*Mic 6:8*
To the weak	*Acts 20:35*
To evangelize	*Matt 9:36–38*

OCCULT

Not to be practiced	*Lev 19:26–28, 31*
Called sin	*1 Sam 15:23*
Listed among works of the flesh	*Gal 5:20*
To increase before Christ's return	*2 Thess 2:9–12*
Practiced by:	
The Babylonians	*Isa 47:9–13*
Belshazzar	*Dan 5:7, 15*

False prophets	Matt 24:24; Jer 14:14
Astrologers	Jer 10:2
Persons converted from:	
Simon Magus	Acts 9:13
Many burned their books	Acts 19:18–19

OFFERING (See also Altar, Sacrifice, Tithe)

Willingly brought	Exod 35:29
Sacrificial	2 Sam 24:24; Isa 53:10
Of Christ to God	Eph 5:2; Heb 9:14
In righteousness	Mal 3:3
According to one's ability	1 Cor 16:1–2
Of body to God	Rom 12:1

OIL (See also Anointing, Ordination)

For light	Exod 35:14
Anointed for kingship	1 Sam 10:1
Anointed for healing	Mark 6:13; James 5:14
Used in offering	Lev 2:1
Figurative of:	
Gladness	Ps 45:7

OINTMENT (See also Perfume)

Used to anoint Christ	Mark 14:3–9
Preparation for burial	Luke 23:55–56

OLD AGE (See also Longevity)

Honor to those of	Lev 19:32
Rejecting advice from those of	1 Kings 12:8
Fruitfulness in	Ps 92:14

A crown of glory   *Prov 16:31*
Live righteously in   *Titus 2:2–3*
In reference to widows   *1 Tim 5:9–10*

OLIVE

Used to make oil   *Exod 27:20*
Trees for Israel   *Deut 6:11*

OLIVET, MOUNT OF OLIVES

Hill near Jerusalem frequented by Jesus and
  his disciples   *Matt 21:1; 24:3; Mark 11:1; 13:3;*
                                Luke 21:37; John 8:1

OMNIPOTENCE OF GOD *(See also God)*

Belongs to him   *Ps 62:11*
Beyond understanding   *Job 26:14*
Praise for   *Rev 19:6*
Nothing too difficult for   *Gen 18:14*
In virgin birth   *Luke 1:35*
In raising Christ   *Eph 1:19–20*

OMNIPRESENCE OF GOD *(See also God)*

With an individual   *Gen 28:15*
No escape from   *Ps 139:7–10*
Awareness of evil and good   *Prov 15:3*
In heaven and earth   *Jer 23:24*
Close to everyone   *Acts 17:27*

OMNISCIENCE OF GOD *(See also God)*

Regarding the heart of man   *Ps 44:21*

Regarding the words of man	Ps 139:4
Is infinite understanding	Ps 147:5
Sees all	Heb 4:13
Beyond man's understanding	Rom 11:33–36

ONESIMUS

| Former slave of Philemon for whom Paul requested freedom | Philem 1–21 |

ONESIPHORUS

| Came to Paul's aid in Rome | 2 Tim 1:16–17 |

OPPORTUNITY *(See also Decision)*

To do good	Gal 6:10
Making the most of	Col 4:5
For salvation	2 Cor 6:2
For evangelism	John 4:35
Used for evil	Matt 26:16
To hear God's voice	1 Sam 3:2–10

OPPRESSION *(See also Affliction, Bondage)*

Not to be guilty of	Lev 25:14
Deliverance from	Ps 72:4
Commanded to relieve	Isa 1:17
Of poor and needy	Amos 4:1; 5:11
By Satan	Acts 10:38
Plea for deliverance from	Ps 119:134

ORDINATION *(See also Anointing)*

| Of a prophet | Jer 1:5–10 |

Of the disciples   *Mark 3:14*
Of the powers of the state   *Rom 13:1*
Of a preacher and apostle   *1 Tim 2:7*
Of elders   *Titus 1:5*

ORPHAN *(See also Adoption)*

Not to afflict   *Exod 22:22*
God helper of   *Ps 10:14*
Finds mercy   *Hos 14:3*
God against those who oppress   *Mal 3:5*
Command to look after   *James 1:27*
Provide food for   *Deut 14:29*

OVERCOMING *(See also Battle, Victory)*

The wicked one   *1 John 2:13*
The world   *John 16:33*
Evil with good   *Rom 12:21*
The corruption of world   *2 Pet 2:20*
Rewarded for   *Rev 2:7, 11, 17, 26; 3:5, 12, 21*

P

PAIN *(See also Adversity, Affliction, Suffering)*

Christ suffered   *Matt 27:27–31, 45–50*
Paul suffered   *2 Cor 11:23–29*
Abolition of   *Rev 21:4*

PARABLE *(See also Allegory)*

Listening to   *Ps 49:4*

Purpose of	Matt 13:13–17
Of the net	Matt 13:47–52
Of mustard seed	Mark 4:30–32
Of the sower	Luke 8:4–15
Of lost sheep, coin, and son	Luke 15

PARADISE (See also Heaven)

Promised by Jesus	Luke 23:43
One caught up into	2 Cor 12:3–4
Incorruptible inheritance in	1 Pet 1:4
Tree of life in	Rev 2:7
Reward great in	Luke 6:23

PARDON (See also Forgiveness, Mercy)

Of sin	Mic 7:18
Prayer for	Ps 25:11
Of one another	Eph 4:32
Refusal to	Matt 18:28–35
Promise of	Isa 55:7
Withheld	Exod 23:21

PARENTS (See also Family, Motherhood)

To be honored by children	Exod 20:12
To be provided for	1 Tim 5:8
Betrayed by	Luke 21:16
To have obedient children	1 Tim 3:4
Grieving	2 Sam 18:33
Providing for children	2 Cor 12:14

PARTIALITY *(See also Justice)*

Commanded not to show	1 Tim 5:21; James 2:1–7
Not an attribute of wisdom	James 3:17
Of parent for child	Gen 37:3
With regard to the poor	Lev 19:15
God does not show	1 Pet 1:17
With regard to salvation	Gal 3:26–29

PASSOVER *(See also Feast, Communion)*

Institution of	Exod 12
And the Last Supper	Matt 26:19; Luke 22:15
An act of faith	Heb 11:28
Lamb of, type of Christ	1 Cor 5:7

PASTOR *(See also Elder, Minister)*

Given the gift of	Eph 4:11
To be a shepherd	1 Pet 5:2–3
Commanded to preach	2 Tim 4:1–2
To pray and minister	Acts 6:4

PATIENCE *(See also Impatience, Long-suffering, Waiting)*

Waiting for the Lord	Ps 130:5
Produced by trubulation	Rom 5:3
Need of	Heb 10:36
Holy Spirit produces	Gal 5:22
Of God for the unrepentant	2 Pet 3:9

PATRIOTISM *(See also Nation, Treason)*

Of a centurion	Luke 7:2–5

Paul appeals to   *2 Cor 11:22*

PAUL *(See also Apostle)*
Conversion of   *Acts 9:1–19*
Claims apostleship   *Gal 1:1, 11–12*
Imprisoned for Christ   *Phil 1:12–13*
Minister of the gospel   *Col 1:23*

PEACE *(See also Contentment, Quiet, Rest)*
God of   *Phil 4:9*
With one another   *Mark 9:50*
Fruit of the Spirit   *Gal 5:22*
Of God   *Phil 4:7*
Of Christ   *John 14:27*
None for the wicked   *Isa 57:21*

PEACE OFFERING *(See also Offering, Sacrifice)*
Sacrifice of   *Lev 3:1*
Commanded to make   *Exod 20:24*
To be offered in Canaan   *Deut 27:1–7*

PENIEL
Where Jacob wrestled with the angel   *Gen 32:30*

PENITENCE *(See also Confession, Remorse)*
Prayer of   *Ps 51*
Joy in heaven over   *Luke 15:7*
God's goodness leads to   *Rom 2:4*
Godly sorrow brings   *2 Cor 7:10*
Example of   *Luke 18:9–14*

PENTECOST, DAY OF *(See also Holy Spirit)*

Coming of Holy Spirit	*Acts 2:1–12*
Amazement on	*Acts 2:5–12*
Peter's sermon on	*Acts 2:14–36*

PERDITION *(See also Hell, Punishment)*

Son of	*John 17:12; 2 Thess 2:3*
Of ungodly men	*2 Pet 3:7*

PERFECTION *(See also Sanctification)*

Growing toward	*Heb 6:1*
Prayer for	*2 Cor 13:9*
Requirements for	*Matt 19:21*
Limit of	*Ps 119:96*

PERFUME *(See also Ointment)*

Rejoices the heart	*Prov 27:9*
Poured upon Christ	*Mark 14:3*
For making incense	*Exod 30:35*

PERSECUTION *(See also Accusation, False; Suffering)*

By friends	*Job 19:22*
Deliverance from	*Ps 7:1–2*
Pray for those guilty of	*Rom 12:14, 19–21*
Against the church	*Acts 11:19*
Promise of	*2 Tim 3:12*

PERSEVERANCE *(See also Long-suffering, Steadfastness)*

In chasing the enemy	*Judg 8:4*

In practicing forgiveness	Matt 18:21–22
Until the end	Mark 13:13
In well-doing	Gal 6:9
In prayer	Eph 6:18

PERSON *(See also Man)*

| No partiality of | Gal 2:6 |
| Of Christ in God's image | Heb 1:3 |

PESTILENCE *(See also Locust, Plague)*

Prayer for deliverance from	1 Kings 8:37–39
Not to be feared	Ps 91:5–6
Coming of	Matt 24:7
Sent by God	Amos 4:10
Upon the disobedient	Jer 42:21–22

PETER *(See also Apostle, Pentecost)*

Brought to Christ and renamed	John 1:40–42
Called to be a disciple	Matt 4:18–20
Walked on the water	Matt 14:22–33
Confessed Jesus as Messiah	Matt 16:13–17
Prophecy concerning later role	Matt 16:18–19
Rebuked	Matt 16:21–23
Failed to understand Christ	John 13:7–11
Denied knowing Jesus	Matt 26:69–75
Witnessed empty tomb	John 20:1–9
Preached at Pentecost	Acts 2:14–41
Healed a beggar	Acts 3:1–10
Leader in early church	Acts 5:1–16; 15:7–14
Ministry to Gentiles	Acts 10:1–11:18

Rebuked by Paul   *Gal 2:11–21*
Commended Paul   *2 Pet 3:15–16*

PHARAOH *(See also Egypt)*

King of Egypt   *Gen 41:46*
Dream of interpreted by Joseph   *Gen 41:25–36*
Named Joseph a ruler   *Gen 41:39–41*

PHARISEES *(See also Sadducees, Sanhedrin)*

At John's baptism   *Matt 3:7–8*
Questioning Jesus   *Mark 7:5*
Attitude toward tax collectors   *Luke 5:30*
Believers who were   *Acts 15:5*

PHILEMON

Slave owner of Onesimus   *Philem 1–25*

PHILIP *(See also Apostle)*

Listed as an apostle   *Matt 10:3*
Called by Christ   *John 1:43*
Preached in Samaria   *Acts 8:5–6*
Witnessed to official   *Acts 8:26–39*

PHILIPPI

Paul persecuted there   *Acts 16:12*
Paul's letter to church   *Phil 1:1–4:23*

PHILISTINES *(See also David, Joshua)*

Abimelech, king of   *Gen 26:8*
Captured Samson   *Judg 16:21*

Captured the ark of God   *1 Sam 5:1–2*
Fought against Israel   *1 Chron 10:1*
Lord will destroy   *Jer 47:4*

PHILOSOPHY *(See also Knowledge, Wisdom)*
Schools of Greek   *Acts 17:18*
Warning against deceptive   *Col 2:8*
Not enough for salvation   *1 Cor 1:20–25; 2:6–10*

PHYSICIAN *(See also Health, Medicine)*
Luke, the beloved   *Col 4:14*
No help from   *Mark 5:26*
For those who are sick   *Mark 2:17*

PILATE
Pontius, governor of Judah   *Luke 3:1*
Examined Jesus   *Matt 27:1–2, 11–26*

PILLAR
Of salt   *Gen 19:26*
Of cloud and fire   *Exod 13:21*
Of the temple   *1 Kings 7:13–22*
Figurative:
Of the church   *1 Tim 3:15*
Of leaders of the church   *Gal 2:9*

PITY *(See also Compassion, Sympathy)*
Upon the poor   *Prov 19:17*
For one another   *1 Pet 3:8*
Of God for his people   *Joel 2:18*

PLAGUE *(See also Pestilence)*

Against the Egyptians	*Exod 9:14; 11:1*
Of leprosy	*Lev 13:2*
Protection from	*Ps 91:10*
Figurative of death	*Hos 13:14*

PLAN OF SALVATION *(See also Salvation)*

Need for	*Rom 3:9–12, 23*
God made known his	*Luke 2:8–11; John 3:16–17*
Christ made possible the	*Rom 5:6; 1 Pet 2:24*
Summary of	*1 Cor 15:3–8; 1 Tim 3:16*

PLEASURE *(See also Amusement, Sensuality)*

At God's right hand	*Ps 16:11*
Of the rich condemned	*James 5:5*
Of creation to God	*Rev 4:11*
Wicked approve of	*Rom 1:32*
In unrighteousness	*2 Thess 2:12*

POETRY *(See also Art)*
Illustrations of:

A psalm of praise	*Ps 136*
Song of Mary	*Luke 1:46–55*
Song of the angels	*Luke 2:14*

POLITICS *(See also Alliance, Compromise, Government)*

Of convenience	*Luke 23:12*
For gain	*Acts 24:26*
Bribery in	*1 Sam 8:3*

Crooked   *Acts 25:7–9*

POLYGAMY *(See also Marriage)*

In Cain's line	*Gen 4:23*
David's	*2 Sam 5:13*
Solomon's	*1 Kings 11:1–3*

POOR PEOPLE *(See also Charity, Justice, Welfare)*

Protection of	*Isa 14:30*
Blessings on	*Luke 6:20*
Provision for	*Ps 58:10*
The righteous understand	*Prov 29:7*
Among believers	*Rev 2:9*

POSSESSIONS *(See Money, Property, Prosperity)*

POTIPHAR

Joseph's master in Egypt	*Gen 39:1–6*
His wife's attempt to seduce Joseph	*Gen 39:6–20*

POTTERY

Molding of	*Jer 18:3–4*
Making, symbol of God's creative work	*Isa 64:8*
Breaking, symbol of god's judgment	*Jer 19:10–11*

POVERTY *(See also Beggar, Riches)*

Can result from:

Too much sleep	*Prov 20:13; 24:33*
Too much drinking or eating	*Prov 23:21*

POWER *(See also Omnipotence, Strength)*

Spirit to give	*Acts 1:8*
Spirit of	*2 Tim 1:7*
God gives to the weak	*Isa 40:29*
Of God	*1 Chron 29:11*
Of Christ	*Matt 28:18*
Over the enemy	*Luke 10:19*

PRAISE *(See also Prayer, Thanksgiving, Worship)*

Of self	*Prov 27:2*

To God:

Because He is worthy	*2 Sam 22:4; Eph 1:6*
In manner of living	*Eph 1:12*
Continually	*Heb 13:15*
Angels singing	*Luke 2:13–14*
With instruments	*Ps 150*

PRAYER *(See also Intercession, Lord's Prayer, Worship)*

Plea for God's attention	*Ps 64:1*
Of the righteous	*Prov 15:29*
Of faith	*James 5:15*
For forgiveness	*Ps 51:1–9*
Continuing in	*Col 4:2*
Hindrance to	*1 Pet 3:7*
Of Christ	*John 17*

PREACHING *(See also Pastor, Sermon, Teaching)*

Entrusted to man by God	*Titus 1:2–3*
Power of God in	*1 Cor 1:18*
Of the disciples	*Luke 9:6*

About Christ's death	*1 Cor 1:23*
To all the world	*Luke 24:47*
Of Peter	*Acts 2:14–36*
Of Paul	*Acts 13:16–41*

PREDESTINATION *(See also Election)*

According to God's purpose	*Rom 8:28–30*
According to his will	*Eph 1:11*
Of Christ's death	*Acts 2:23*

PREGNANCY *(See also Baby)*

God forms unborn child	*Ps 139:13–16*
Of Eve, the first to conceive	*Gen 4:1*
Of Sarah in her old age	*Gen 21:1–2*
Of Elizabeth in her old age	*Luke 1:24, 57*
Of Hannah, who prayed for a son	*1 Sam 1:11*
Of Mary	*Matt 1:20–25; Luke 1:31–34*

PRESENCE OF GOD *(See also Glory, God, Majesty)*

Hiding from	*Gen 3:8*
Appearance of	*Num 20:6*
Joy in	*Ps 16:11*
Coming to with praise	*Ps 100:1–2*
Brings conviction of sin	*Isa 6:1–7*

PRESUMPTION *(See also Arrogance, Disobedience, Pride)*

Sins of	*Ps 19:13*
Ignoring authority	*2 Pet 2:10*
Sinning purposefully	*Num 15:30*

A prophet speaking falsely   *Deut 18:22*

PRIDE *(See also Arrogance, Boasting, Conceit)*

Before a fall   *Prov 16:18*
Origin of   *1 John 2:16*
Deceptiveness of   *Jer 49:16*
Of the wicked   *Ps 10:4*
Warning against   *Rom 12:3*

PRIEST *(See also Aaron, Chief Priest, Priesthood)*

Converted   *Acts 6:7*
Jesus as:
  Appointed by God   *Heb 5:5*
  Appointed forever   *Heb 5:6*
  Intercessor   *Rom 8:34*
  Is able to sympathize   *Heb 4:14*
  He is faithful   *Heb 2:17*
The Christian as:
  Worshiper   *1 Peter 2:5*
  To God   *Rev 1:6*

PRIESTHOOD *(See also Aaron, Priest, Offering)*

Of Aaron   *Exod 28:1; Heb 5:1–5*
Of Melchizedek   *Gen 14:18; Ps 110:4*
Of Christ   *Heb 4:14; 5:5–10; 7:24*
Of believers   *1 Pet 2:5*

PRISCILLA

Wife of Aquila, co-worker with Paul   *Acts 18:1–3*

PRISON *(See also Captivity, Liberty, Prisoner)*

Satan freed from	Rev 20:7
Paul's witness in	Eph 6:20
Willingness to go to	Luke 22:33
Peter freed from	Acts 12:6–10

PRISONER *(See also Bondage, Prison)*

For Christ	Phil 1:13–14
Of hope	Zech 9:12
Lord's promise for	Isa 42:7
Mistreatment of	Isa 20:4

PROFANITY *(See also Blasphemy, Swearing)*

Using God's name falsely	Lev 19:12; 1 Cor 12:3
As blasphemy	Rom 2:24; James 2:7
Not to be practiced	Col 3:8; James 3:10; 5:12
The Law forbids	Exod 20:7

PROMISE *(See also Covenant, Testament, Vow)*

Of God	Titus 1:2; Heb 10:23
In Christ	Eph 2:13; 3:6
Of Christ to disciples	John 14
Gentiles share in	Eph 3:6

PROPERTY *(See also Money)*

Rich in	Gen 30:43
Coveting	Luke 12:15–21

PROPHECY *(See also Prophet)*

Gift of	Rom 12:6; 1 Cor 12:10

Origin in the Holy Spirit   2 Peter 1:21
To be heeded   1 Thess 5:20; 2 Pet 1:19
Associated with a vision   Dan 9:21–27

PROPHET *(See also Prophetess, Revelation)*

Appointed by God   Jer 1:5–9
God's instrument   Hos 12:13
Receiving of   Matt 10:41
Without honor at home   Matt 13:57
Examples of:
Moses   Deut 34:10
Isaiah   Matt 3:3; 15:7
Ezekiel   Ezek 3:4

PROPHETESS *(See also Prophet)*

Examples of:
Miriam   Exod 15:20
Deborah   Judg 4:4
Huldah   2 Kings 22:14
Anna   Luke 2:36

PROPITIATION *(See also Atonement, Sacrifice)*

Demonstration of God's justice   Rom 3:25
Christ dying for sin   1 John 2:2
Act of God's love   1 John 4:10

PROSPERITY *(See also Blessing, Riches)*

Peril of   Luke 12:13–21
Basing life on   Ps 52:6–7
Of the unrighteous   Ps 73:12

PROSTITUTION *(See also Lust, Sexual Conduct)*

Avoiding	*Prov 5:8; Rom 13:14; 1 Thess 4:3*
Leads to hell	*Prov 5:5*

PROTECTION

Of man by God:

In time of trouble	*Ps 46:1; Jer 16:19*
In time of evil	*Jer 17:17*
When no one cares	*Ps 142:4*

PROVERB *(See also Wisdom)*

Purpose of	*Prov 1:2–6*
Understanding of	*Prov 1:6*
Solomon's use of many	*1 Kings 4:29–32*
Quoted by Jesus	*Luke 4:23*

PROVIDENCE *(See also Sovereignty)*

For the earth	*Gen 8:22; Matt 5:45*
For believers	*Matt 6:33; 10:28–31*
For salvation	*Luke 2:10–11; 2 Pet 3:9*

PRUDENCE *(See also Acting Wisely, Discretion, Wisdom)*

Wisdom dwells with	*Prov 8:12*
Brings knowledge	*Prov 14:18*
Involves silence at times	*Amos 5:13*
Solomon's gift of	*2 Chron 2:12*

PSALMS *(See also Hymn, Music)*

Of encouragement	*Col 3:16*

Of thanksgiving	Ps 95:2
Of praise	Ps 104
Of prayer	Ps 102
Singing of	1 Chron 16:9; James 5:13

PUBLICAN, TAX COLLECTOR (See also Taxes)

Jesus eating with	Matt 9:11
Humble prayer of	Luke 18:13
Levi	Luke 5:27

PUNISHMENT (See also Condemnation, Damnation, Wrath)

Of children	Prov 13:24; 19:18
Eternal	Matt 25:46; Rev 20:14–15
Of evildoers	1 Pet 2:14
Of angels	Jude 6

PURIFICATION (See also Purity, Washing)

Of leper	Lev 14:2
From sin	Ps 51:7
By the Word	Ps 119:11; Eph 5:26
By Christ's blood	1 John 1:7
Symbolic, of one another	John 13:5–15

PURITY (See also Chastity, Cleanliness, Sanctification)

Is blessed	Matt 5:8
In a corrupt world	Phil 2:14–15
Think on	Phil 4:8

Q

QUARREL *(See also Arguing, Fighting)*

Caused by drunkenness	*Prov 23:29–30*
Preventing	*Phil 2:14*
False teachers indulging in	*1 Tim 6:3–5*
Example of	*Acts 15:36–39*

QUEEN *(See also King)*

Of Sheba	*1 Kings 10:1*
Vashti	*Esther 1:9*
Esther	*Esther 7:2*
Of heaven	*Jer 44:17, 25*
Candace	*Acts 8:27*

QUIET *(See also Peace)*

Better than toil	*Eccles 4:6*
Strength in	*Isa 30:15*
Of the sea	*Mark 4:39*
In heaven	*Rev 8:1*
Before the Lord	*Hab 2:20*

QUIET TIME *(See also Meditation, Prayer)*

To study his Word	*2 Tim 3:16–17*
To pray:	
In the Spirit	*Eph 6:18*
Giving thanks	*1 Thess 5:18*
With the mind	*1 Cor 14:15*
For help in temptation	*Mark 14:38*

For forgiveness of sin   *1 John 1:9*
To praise God:
For his love and goodness   *Ps 107:1*
For what he has done   *Ps 111:1–9*

R

RABBI *(See also Minister, Teacher)*
Christ the true   *Matt 23:8*
Term of respect:
Used by disciples   *John 1:38; 6:25*
Used by Nicodemus   *John 3:2*

RACE
Christian life compared to   *1 Cor 9:24; Heb 12:1*
Renewed strength for   *Isa 40:31*
Patiently running   *Heb 12:1*

RACHEL
Daughter of Laban   *Gen 29:10*
Jacob"s love for   *Gen 29:17–18, 20*
Death of   *Gen 35:19*
Sons of   *Gen 35:24*

RACISM *(See also Bigotry, Intolerance)*
Paul speaking against   *Rom 3:9–10; Gal 3:28*
Jesus speaking against   *Luke 9:49–50; 18:9–14*
Instances of:
By Israelites   *Ps 65:5*

By Joshua	*Num 11:26–29*
By Pharisees	*Luke 7:39*
By Samaritans	*John 4:9*
By early Christians	*Acts 10:45*

RAHAB

Harlot who hid Israelite spies	*Josh 2:1–21; 6:22*
Commended for her faith	*Heb 11:31; James 2:25*

RAIN *(See also Cloud)*

The Flood	*Gen 7:12*
Withheld as punishment	*1 Kings 8:35–36; 17:1*
Sent by God	*Job 5:8–10; Matt 5:45*

RAINBOW *(See also Noah)*

God's promise	*Gen 9:12–16*
In Ezekiel's vision	*Ezek 1:28*
Around the throne	*Rev 4:3*
On an angel's head	*Rev 10:1*

RAMAH

Home of Samuel	*1 Sam 1:19–20; 7:15–17*

RANSOM *(See also Redemption, Atonement)*

Christ's death as	*Mark 10:45; 1 Tim 2:5–6*

RAPE

Death penalty for	*Deut 22:25–27*
Of Tamar by Amnon	*2 Sam 13:6–33*
Of Dinah	*Gen 34:2*

REASONING *(See also Knowledge, Wisdom)*

Job and friends	*Job 13:6*
God and the sinner	*Isa 1:18*
In public praying and speaking	*1 Cor 14:13–19*
Without considering God	*James 4:13–17*

REBECCA *(See also Isaac)*

Wife of Isaac	*Gen 24:67*
Plotting by	*Gen 27:5–6*
Burial	*Gen 49:31*

REBELLION *(See also Disobedience)*

Of Israel against God	*1 Sam 8:4–9*
Of Saul	*1 Sam 15:22–23*
Of mankind	*Rom 1:18–32*
Of angels	*Jude 6*
Of Satan	*Isa 14:12–15*

RECONCILIATION *(See also Fellowship)*

To brother	*Matt 5:23–24; 18:15–17*
To God by Christ's death	*Rom 5:10–11*
Of whole creation	*Col 1:19–20*

RED SEA *(See also Exodus)*

Miraculous parting of	*Exod 14:21*
Crossing of	*Exod 14:22*
Destruction of Egyptians in	*Exod 14:26–28*

REDEEMER *(See also Jesus Christ, Redemption)*

Job's faith in	*Job 19:25*

David's prayer to   *Ps 19:14*
Is strong   *Jer 50:34*
Of Israel   *Isa 49:7*
Defends orphans   *Prov 23:1*

REDEMPTION *(See also Cross, Ransom)*

In Christ Jesus   *Rom 3:24*
Christ our   *1 Cor 1:30; Eph 1:17; 4:30*
Sent by God   *Ps 111:9*
Of all creation   *Rom 8:19–23*

REGENERATION *(See also Conversion, Salvation)*

Spiritual rebirth   *Titus 3:5*
Produces new nature   *Col 3:10*
By the Word of God   *1 Pet 1:23*
Required   *John 3:3*

REHOBOAM

King of Judah   *1 Kings 11:43–12:1; 14:21–31*
His conflict with Jeroboam   *1 Kings 12:1–19; 14:30*

REJOICING *(See also Happiness, Joy)*

Because of:
God's salvation   *Rom 15:13*
God's creation   *Isa 65:18*
Jesus' birth   *Matt 2:10*
The repentance of sinners   *Luke 15:7*
Hope in Christ   *Rom 12:12*

RELATIONSHIP *(See also Behavior, Family, Friendship)*

Of believers as children of God	*Rom 8:16*
Of believers with one another	*1 Cor 12:12–14, 26*
Of believers with Christ:	
Rooted in Him	*Col 2:7*
Fellow heirs with	*Rom 8:17*
Of believers with Holy Spirit:	
Indwelt by	*Rom 8:9*
Taught by	*John 14:26*
Of believers with non-believers:	
Not to marry	*2 Cor 6:14–15*
To be good examples to	*Matt 5:13*
To do good to	*Matt 5:14–16*

RELIGION *(See also God, Salvation)*

Mystery of	*1 Tim 3:16*
Pure	*James 1:26–27*
Without power	*2 Tim 3:8*
True:	
Description of	*Matt 22:36–40; Rom 10:1–13*
Test of	*2 Cor 13:5; 1 John 4:7–21*
Consistency of	*2 Tim 4:7*

REMNANT *(See also Israel)*

God's grace toward	*Isa 1:9*
Prayer for	*Isa 37:4*
Deliverance of	*Mic 2:12*

REMORSE (See also Conviction of Sin, Guilt, Penitence)

Coming too late	*Heb 12:17*

Leads to:

Calling on the Lord	*Ps 41:4*
Recognizing sin	*Luke 15:18*
Confessing sin	*Ps 51:3–4*

RENEWAL (See Revival)

REPENTANCE (See also Conversion, Penitence)

The Lord responds to	*2 Chron 7:14*
Requires humility	*2 Kings 22:19*
In conversion	*Acts 3:19*
By Christians	*Rev 3:3*
Producing fruit	*Luke 3:8*
Producing joy	*Luke 15:7*
To be preached	*Luke 24:47*

REPROOF (See also Discipline)

Provides understanding	*Prov 15:32*
Results in wisdom	*Prov 29:15*
In teaching	*2 Tim 4:2*
In Christian love	*Rev 3:19*
In discipline	*Heb 12:5*

REPUTATION (See also Character, Integrity)

For wisdom	*1 Kings 10:7*
For righteousness	*Prov 18:10*
For faith	*Rom 1:8*

Acceptable before God   *Rom 14:18*

RESENTMENT *(See Anger, Bitterness, Retaliation)*

RESPECT *(See also Honor)*
For government	*Rom 13:7*
Shown by children	*Eph 6:1–2*
Shown by wives	*Eph 5:33*
For all	*1 Pet 2:17*

RESPONSIBILITY *(See also Duty, Obligation)*
To brother	*Gen 4:9*
For sin	*Jer 31:30*
To work for God	*Matt 9:37*
For one's behavior	*Rom 14:12–13*
To teach	*2 Tim 2:2*
To love one another	*1 John 3:16; 4:11*

REST *(See also Peace, Sleep)*
In God:
By trusting	*Ps 37:5*
With confidence	*1 Pet 1:21*
None for the rebellious	*Heb 3:11*

In Christ:
When troubled	*Matt 11:28*
For the soul	*Ps 116:7*

From work:
God initiated	*Exod 23:12*
Heavenly	*Rev 14:13*

RESTITUTION (See also Justice)

Making full	Exod 22:5–6, 12
Made by oppressor	Job 20:18
At conversion	Luke 19:8

RESTORATION

Example in Abraham's life	Gen 20:14
Of the Kingdom	Acts 1:6–8
Of sinning believer	Gal 6:1
Of the body	Matt 12:13; Mark 8:25

RESURRECTION (See also Crucifixion)

Of Jesus	John 20:1–20
Disciples witness to	Acts 1:22
Hope of believers	Rom 6:5; 1 Cor 15:13, 42
Power experienced	Phil 3:10
Of the righteous dead	Rev 20:5–6

RETALIATION (See also Revenge)

With evil prohibited	Rom 12:17; 1 Pet 3:9

RETARDED

Not exempt from heaven	Matt 19:13–14

REUBEN

Firstborn of Jacob	Gen 29:32
Inheritance of descendants	Josh 13:15–23

REVELATION *(See also Inspiration, Mystery, Scripture)*

Through prophets	*Deut 18:18*
All to be known	*Mark 4:22*
Through Jesus	*John 15:15*
By the Spirit	*1 Cor 2:10; Eph 3:1–6*

REVENGE *(See also Retaliation, Vengeance)*

Example of	*Gen 34:1–31*

As God's responsibility:

Against the enemy	*Deut 32:41; Prov 20:22*
Prohibited	*Rom 12:19*
Against evil	*Rom 13:4*

REVERENCE *(See also Awe, Fear, Worship)*

Shown to God	*Exod 3:5*
To God above all	*1 Chron 16:25; Job 36:26*
Towards Christ	*1 Pet 3:15*

REVIVAL *(See also Holy Spirit)*

Accomplished by God	*Ps 51:10; 80:7*
Through His Word	*Ps 119:25*
Of the soul	*Ps 19:7*

REWARD *(See also Blessing, Judgment)*

Given by God	*Matt 6:6*

Given for:

Showing love	*Matt 10:42*
Perseverance	*Phil 3:14; James 1:12*
Righteousness	*2 Tim 4:8*

Suffering   *2 Tim 2:12*

RICHES *(See also Abundance, Money, Poverty)*
Source of   *Deut 8:18*
Abuse of   *Prov 28:20*
Futility of   *Matt 6:19; Luke 12:20*
Spiritual   *Acts 3:6; Eph 3:8*
As a hindrance   *Mark 10:24; Luke 6:24*

RIDICULE *(See Mocking)*

RIGHTEOUS, THE *(See also Righteousness)*
God   *Ps 7:11*
Jesus Christ   *1 John 2:1*
Eternal life for   *Matt 25:46*
God's care over   *1 Pet 3:12*
Are fruitful   *Ps 92:12–14*
Afflictions of   *Ps 34:19*

RIGHTEOUSNESS *(See also Godliness, Justice, Justification)*
Of God   *Rom 1:17; 3:21*
Of sinners   *Isa 64:6*
God loves   *Ps 33:5*
Of Christ   *1 Cor 1:30*
Persecuted for   *Matt 5:10*
Kingdom of God is   *Rom 14:17*
In new heavens and new earth   *2 Pet 3:13*

RIVER

| In the city of God | Ps 46:4 |

Likened to:

Life	Ps 1:3; Rev 22:1
Prosperity	Isa 66:12
Place of safety	Isa 33:21

ROAD *(See also Way)*

| The way of the Lord | Deut 5:33; 1 Sam 12:23 |
| Blessings of walking in the Lord's ways | Ps 128:1 |

ROBBERY *(See also Thief)*

Command against	Exod 20:15
Of the poor	Prov 22:22
Of the Father's house	Jer 7:11
Of neighbors	Lev 19:13
Causes destruction	John 10:10

ROCK *(See also Foundation)*

Christ the	1 Cor 10:4; 1 Pet 2:4
Source of water for Israel	Isa 48:21
Figuratively, of the body of Christ	1 Pet 2:5
House built on	Matt 7:24
Tomb hewn out of	Mark 15:46

ROMAN EMPIRE *(See also Rome)*

Ruled by Caesars	Luke 2:1; Phil 4:21
Taxed by	Luke 2:1
Paul was citizen of	Acts 22:27–29
Paul's defense in court of	Acts 25:10

ROME *(See also Roman Empire)*

Paul imprisoned at	*Acts 28:17, 30*
Church of	*Rom 1:7*
Paul's desire to visit church at	*Rom 1:10–11*
Paul's desire to preach the gospel at	*Rom 1:15*

RULER *(See also King, Palace, Throne)*

Evil	*Eph 6:12*
Used in derision	*Acts 7:27*
Ultimately God	*2 Kings 19:15*
Authority given to man	*Gen 1:26*

RUTH

Widow devoted to mother-in-law	*Ruth 1:16–17, 22*
Gathered grain in Boaz's field	*Deut 24:19; Ruth 2:2*
Married Boaz	*Ruth 4:13*

S

SABBATH *(See also Lord's Day)*

Its holiness	*Exod 20:8*
For rest	*Lev 16:31*
Blessing in keeping it	*Isa 56:2*
Profaning of	*Ezek 22:8*
Jesus is Lord of	*Matt 12:8*
Made for man	*Mark 2:27*

SACRIFICE *(See also Altar, Animal, Offering)*

Of Christ for sin	*Heb 9:26*

Love more important than	Mark 12:33
Lives acceptable to God	Rom 12:1
Loss for Christ	Phil 3:7–8

SADDUCEES *(See also Pharisees, Sanhedrin)*

Tempting Jesus	Matt 16:1
Teaching of	Matt 16:11
Sayings of	Matt 16:2
Against teaching of the resurrection	Acts 4:1–2; 23:7

SAFETY *(See Protection, Security)*

SAINT *(See also Holiness, Sanctification)*

Called of God	Rom 1:7; 1 Cor 1:2
Immorality not fitting	Eph 5:3
Any member of God's family	Eph 2:19
God will not forsake	Ps 37:28

SALT

As a seasoning	Job 6:6
Figurative:	
Of believer	Matt 5:13
Speech seasoned with	Col 4:6

SALVATION *(See also Deliverance, Plan of Salvation)*

Through Christ	Gal 1:4; 2 Tim 1:9–10
Gift of God	John 3:16; Rom 6:23
By faith	Luke 7:50; Eph 2:8
Working it out with fear	Phil 2:12
God's plan for	1 Thess 5:9–10; 2 Pet 3:9

Now is day of   *2 Cor 6:2*
Completion of   *Rom 13:11*

SAMARIA *(See also Israel°)*

Capital of Israel   *1 Kings 16:24–29*
Threatened with judgment   *Isa 28:1–4*
Churches established in   *Acts 9:31*
Jesus talked with woman of   *John 4:7–30*

SAMSON *(See also Judges of Israel)*

Blessed of the Lord at birth   *Judg 13:24*
Had great strength from God   *Judg 15:14–15*
Lost his strength   *Judg 16:15–17, 19*
Imprisoned by his enemies   *Judg 16:21*
Enabled to avenge his enemies   *Judg 16:28–30*

SAMUEL

Son of Elkanah and Hannah   *1 Sam 1:19, 26*
The Lord spoke to him while a youth   *1 Sam 3:11*
Judge of Israel   *1 Sam 7:3–8:22*
Anointed Saul king   *1 Sam 10:1*
Rebuked Saul for sin   *1 Sam 13:13*
Anointed David king   *1 Sam 16:1–13*
His faith commended   *Ps 99:6; Acts 3:24; Heb 11:32*

SANCTIFICATION *(See also Consecration, Holiness, Justification)*

Of believers in Christ   *1 Cor 1:2; 6:11; Heb 10:10, 14*
By Christ's power   *Phil 3:21*
Through faith   *Acts 26:18*

| Through the Spirit | 1 Pet 1:2 |
| Willed by God | 1 Thess 4:3 |

SANCTUARY (See also Holy Place, Tabernacle)

Lord's dwelling place	Gen 28:16; Ps 11:4
Beauty of	Ps 96:6
Holiness of	1 Cor 3:17
To be revered	Lev 19:30; John 2:16

SANHEDRIN (See also Pharisees, Sadducees)

Jesus' appearance before	Luke 22:66; John 18:19
Apostles' appearance before	Acts 6:27
Gamaliel, a member of	Acts 5:34

SANITATION (See also Cleanliness, Purity)
Commands regarding:

Washing	Deut 23:10–11
Burning	Num 31:19–23
Covering filth	Deut 23:12
Dead bodies	Lev 11:24–40
Leprosy	Lev 13:2–59
Human discharge	Lev 15:1–30

SAPPHIRA (See Ananias)

SARAH (See also Abraham)

Wife of Abraham	Gen 11:29
Called Abraham's sister	Gen 12:10–20
Gave birth to a son in her old age	Gen 21:2

SATAN *(See also Demon, Devil, Evil)*

As the serpent	*Gen 3:4*
Responsible for Job's suffering	*Job 1:6–12; 2:1–7*
Temptation of Jesus by	*Matt 4:1–11*
God of this world	*2 Cor 4:4*
Adversary of believers	*1 Pet 5:8*
Power of contrasted with God's power	*Acts 26:18*
To be tormented forever	*Rev 20:10*

SAUL, KING

Anointing of	*1 Sam 11:6*
Tried to kill David	*1 Sam 19:1–10*
Committed suicide	*1 Sam 31:4*

SAUL OF TARSUS *(See Paul)*

SAVIOR *(See also Jesus Christ)*

Identified as God	*Ps 106:21*
Applied to Christ	*2 Tim 1:10*
Believed to be	*John 4:42*

Described by:

Prophets	*Isa 42:6–7*
Angels	*Matt 1:20–21*
John the Baptist	*John 1:29*
Peter	*Acts 5:31*
Paul	*1 Tim 1:15*
John	*1 John 4:14*

SCAPEGOAT *(See also Sacrifice)*

Presented alive	*Lev 16:10, 20–22*

SCEPTER *(See also Ruler)*

Symbol of authority from Israel	*Num 24:17*
Extended by King	*Esther 5:2*
Symbol of righteousness	*Heb 1:8*

SCHOOL *(See also Teacher)*

In home	*Deut 6:6–9*
Music training for temple	*1 Chron 25:1–8*

SCOFF, SCOFFERS *(See also Mocking)*

Appearing in the last days	*2 Pet 3:3*
Blind man abused by	*John 9:28*
At Pentecost	*Acts 2:13*
Questions by	*Ps 42:10; 73:11; 78:19*

SCRIBE *(See also Law, Pharisees, Writing)*

Instructor of Law	*Matt 7:29*
Lacked righteousness	*Matt 5:20*
Jesus warned	*Mark 12:38–40*
Wisdom of, was foolish	*1 Cor 1:20*
Jesus suffered at hands of	*Matt 16:21*

SCRIPTURE *(See also Inspiration, Revelation, Word of God)*

Given by God	*2 Tim 3:16*
Inspired by Holy Spirit	*Acts 1:16; 2 Pet 1:21*
Christ taught	*Luke 24:27*
For instruction	*Rom 15:4*
Bears witness to Christ	*John 5:39–40*
To cleanse	*Eph 5:26*

Called Sword of the Spirit	*Eph 6:17*
Likened to a lamp	*2 Pet 1:19*
Presents way of salvation	*2 Tim 3:15*

SEA *(See also Red Sea)*

Pharaoh and his army destroyed in	*Exod 15:4*
Jesus walking beside	*Matt 4:18*
Gives up dead at judgment	*Rev 20:13*

SEAL

Of righteousness	*Rom 4:11*
Of apostleship	*1 Cor 9:2*
Of Holy Spirit	*2 Cor 1:22*
Christ worthy to open	*Rev 5:9*

SEASON

Origin of	*Gen 1:14*
Change of will continue	*Gen 8:22*
For everything	*Eccles 3:1*

SECOND COMING *(See also Antichrist)*

Signs of	*Matt 24:4–25*
Events of	*Matt 24:26–44; Luke 21:25–28*
Described	*1 Thess 4:13–18*
Foretold	*Acts 1:9–11*
Promise of	*John 14:3*

SECOND DEATH *(See also Hell)*

| To everlasting contempt | *Dan 12:2* |
| To the lake of fire | *Rev 20:14* |

| A resurrection of judgment | John 5:29 |
| To escape from | John 8:51; Rev 2:11 |

SECRET (See also Mystery)

Belongs to the Lord	Deut 29:29
Of men to be judged	Eccles 12:14; Rom 2:16
Sins known by God	Ps 90:8
Deeds exposed	John 3:20
Of the heart revealed	1 Cor 14:25

SECURITY (See also Peace, Protection)

With Christ	Heb 6:19
Of a heavenly body	2 Cor 5:1–5
In the New Earth	Isa 11:6

SELF-ACCEPTANCE (See also Self-examination)
Of believers:

In knowing forgiveness of sins	Col 1:14
In knowing God's acceptance of them	Eph 2:19–22
In recognizing gift	1 Cor 12:4–6, 12–31

SELF-CONTROL (See also Character)

A Christian virtue	2 Pet 1:6
Of Jesus	Matt 27:12–14
Urged in light of Christ's return	1 Thess 5:6

Elements of:

Control of one's body	1 Cor 9:27
Sober judgment	Rom 12:3
Control of one's temper	Prov 16:32

SELF-DEFENSE

Jesus', in his trial	*Mark 15:2–5; Luke 23:3*
Protected under Jewish law	*John 7:51*

SELF-DELUSION *(See also Pride)*

Contributing factors:

Natural wisdom	*Prov 14:12*
False teaching	*1 Thess 5:3*
False view of God	*2 Pet 3:3–5*

SELF-DENIAL *(See also Humility, Self-control)*

Described as:

Denial	*Titus 2:12; 1 Pet 4:2*
Putting to death	*Col 3:5*
Renunciation	*Luke 14:33*
Putting off	*Eph 4:22*
Taking up the cross	*Matt 10:38*

Commended as:

Spiritual worship	*Rom 12:1–2*
Expression of love	*Rom 16:4*
Worthy of reward	*Luke 18:28–30*

SELF-EXAMINATION *(See also Self-acceptance)*

By means of:

God's Word	*Ps 119:59; Heb 4:12*
Christ's example	*Heb 12:1–2*
God himself	*Job 13:23; Ps 26:2; 139:23*

Purposes of:

Preparation for Lord's Supper	*1 Cor 11:28–32*
Test of one's faith	*2 Cor 13:5*

Test of one's works   *Gal 6:4*

SELF-INDULGENCE *(See also Self-control)*
Judged   *Eccles 11:9*
Instances of:
Solomon   *Eccles 2:10; 8:15*
The rich fool   *Luke 12:16–20*

SELFISHNESS *(See also Behavior, Self-indulgence,*
   Submission)
Exemplified in:
Self-love   *2 Tim 3:2*
Self-seeking   *Phil 2:21*
Avoided by:
Service to others   *Rom 15:2–3; 1 Cor 10:24*
Following Christ's example   *Mark 10:43–45*
Submission to Christ   *Phil 1:21*
Manifesting love   *1 Cor 3:5*

SELF-RIGHTEOUSNESS *(See also Humility,*
   Righteousness)
Described as:
Presumptuous   *Deut 9:4–6*
Unprofitable   *Isa 57:12*
Offensive   *Isa 64:6; 65:4*
Outward show   *Matt 23:25–28*
Rejecting God's righteousness   *Rom 10:3*

SELF-WILL *(See also Self-control)*
Revealed in:
Presumption	*Num 14:40–45; Neh 9:16–17*
Rebellious attitude towards parents	*Deut 21:18–21*
Stubbornness	*Isa 48:4–8*

SENSUALITY *(See also Idolatry, Immorality, Pleasure)*
Manifested in divisive, ungodly men	*Jude 18–19*
Associated with worldly wisdom	*James 3:15*
Encouraged if no resurrection	*1 Cor 15:32*

SERAPHIM *(See also Angels, Cherubim)*
Description	*Isa 6:2–7*

SERMON *(See also Preaching, Teaching)*
On the Mount	*Matt 5:7*
Of Peter	*Acts 2:14–36; 3:12–26*
Of Stephen	*Acts 7:2–53*
Of Paul in Athens	*Acts 17:18, 22–31*

SERPENT *(See also Devil)*
In temptation of man	*Gen 3:1–19; 2 Cor 11:3*
Cursed	*Gen 3:14*

Miracles associated with:
Moses' rod	*Exod 4:3; 7:9–10*
Hebrews cured by	*Num 21:8–9*

SERVANT *(See also Bondage, Ministry)*
Christ is:
Of man	*Matt 20:28; Luke 22:27*

Bond-servant   *Phil 2:7–8*

Of Christ:

To be content   *1 Cor 7:20–21*

Paul   *Phil 1:1; Titus 1:1*

Duties:

Honor master   *Mal 1:6; 1 Tim 6:1*

Obey master   *Eph 6:5; Titus 2:9*

SETH

Third son of Adam   *Gen 4:25; 5:3*

SEVEN

Days for Feast of Tabernacles   *Exod 12:15–19*

Day of the week to rest   *Exod 20:10*

The sabbatical year   *Lev 25:2–6*

Times around Jericho   *Josh 6:4*

SEVENTY

Elders to assist Moses   *Num 11:16*

Years in Babylonian exile   *Jer 25:11*

Weeks of redemption   *Dan 9:24*

Times seven   *Matt 18:22*

Jesus sends   *Luke 10:1*

SEXUAL CONDUCT *(See also Celibacy, Lust, Marriage)*

As intercourse   *Gen 4:1*

As union   *Gen 2:24; Exod 22:16; 1 Cor 6:16*

As privilege of marriage   *1 Cor 7:3–5*

Unrighteous out of marriage   *1 Cor 6:9–10*

SHADRACH *(See also Meshach, Abednego)*

Deliverance from furnace   *Dan 1:1–7; 3:1–30*

SHAME *(See also Guilt, Remorse)*

Of Adam and Eve	*Gen 3:7–10*
Of those who disregard God's law	*Hos 4:6–7*
Of those who deny Jesus	*Mark 8:38; Luke 9:26*
Suffered for Christ's sake	*Acts 5:41*
Is glory of enemies of cross	*Phil 3:19*
Of the cross	*Heb 12:2*
Avoid by abiding in Christ	*1 John 2:28*

SHEBA, QUEEN OF

Visited Solomon   *1 Kings 10:1–13*

SHEEP *(See also Animal, Sacrifice)*

Literal:

As sacrifice	*Gen 4:4; 8:20; 22:13*
Jacob cares for	*Gen 30:32–40*

Figurative:

As servants of God	*Ps 100:3; John 21:15–17*
Of mankind	*Isa 53:6*
Of innocence	*Matt 7:15*
Of sinner in parable	*Matt 18:11–13; Luke 15:4–7*

SHEM

Son of Noah   *Gen 5:32; 9:26; 1 Chron 1:17–27*

SHEOL *(See also Death)*

God's anger burns there   *Deut 32:22*

A place of abandonment   Ps 16:10
A place of the dead   Ezek 32:21

SHEPHERD (See also Parable, Pastor)
Duties:
To provide food   Ps 23:2
To watch strays   Matt 18:12
To protect   1 Sam 17:34–35; Amos 3:12
Figurative of:
God's provision   Ps 23; 78:52; 80:1
Prophets and priests   Ezek 34
Jesus   John 10:11; 1 Pet 2:25

SHEWBREAD, SHOWBREAD (See also
Tabernacle)
In tabernacle   Exod 25:30; Lev 24:8
Description of   Lev 24:5–6
As an offering   Lev 24:7
Food for High Priest's family   Lev 24:9
David asked for   1 Sam 21:1–6

SHIELD (See also Armor)
Made of:
Gold   2 Sam 8:7; 1 Kings 10:16
Bronze   1 Kings 14:27
Figurative of:
God   Gen 15:1; Deut 33:29; 2 Sam 22:3
God's faithfulness   Ps 91:4
Faith   Eph 6:16
Salvation   2 Sam 22:36

SHILOH
Site of tabernacle   *Josh 18:1; Judg 21:19*

SHIMEI
Cursed David   *2 Sam 16:5*
Killed by Solomon   *1 Kings 2:36*

SICKNESS *(See also Health, Disease, Medicine)*
Under God's control   *Deut 32:39; 1 Cor 11:30*
Because of sin   *Lev 26:14–16; 2 Chron 21:12–15*
Result of excesses   *Hos 7:5; Prov 25:16*
Christ healed   *Matt 4:23; 8:3, 13; Mark 10:52*
Pray for those in   *Acts 28:8; James 5:14–15*

SIGN *(See also Miracle)*
A distinctive mark:
Of God's work   *Exod 4:28–30; 7:3–5; Acts 2:43*
Of a prophecy   *1 Sam 10:1–8; Isa 7:11–14*
Of God's messenger   *Matt 12:38–40; John 2:11*
Of end times   *Luke 21:11, 25*

SILAS
Leader in Jerusalem sent with Paul   *Acts 15:22*
Imprisoned with Paul at Philippi   *Acts 16:16–40*

SILVER *(See also Gold, Money)*
As money   *Gen 17:12; Matt 10:9*
In tabernacle   *Exod 26:19; Num 7:13*
In temple   *1 Chron 28:14; 29:2–5; Ezra 5:14*

SIMEON

Son of Jacob   *Gen 29:33*
His descendants   *Gen 46:10; Exod 6:15*
Prophesied concerning infant Jesus   *Luke 2:25–35*

SIMON *(See Peter)*

SIN *(See also Guilt, Sinner, Wickedness)*

Known of God   *Gen 3:11; Ps 44:21; 69:5; Matt 10:26*
God's displeasure in   *Gen 6:6; Deut 25:16; Ps 5:4*
Righteous do not condone   *Gen 39:9; Deut 7:26*
Consequences of   *Exod 20:5; Prov 14:11; Rom 5:12*
Forgiveness of   *Exod 34:7; Matt 26:28*
Confession of   *Neh 1:16; James 5:16; 1 John 1:9*
Jesus takes away   *John 1:29; 2 Cor 5:21*

SINAI, MOUNT

Where Commandments were given   *Gen 19:1–25*

SINCERITY *(See also Honesty, Integrity)*

Of forgiveness   *Matt 18:21–22*
Of faith   *1 Tim 1:5*
Of ministers   *Titus 2:7*
Of Jesus   *1 Pet 2:22*
Of Christian love:
For others   *Rom 12:9; 1 Pet 1:22; 1 John 3:18*
For God   *Deut 6:5*
For Christ   *Eph 6:24*

SINGING *(See also Music, Voice)*
Because of rejoicing:

For friend	Gen 31:27
For victory	Exod 15:1
At feasts	Isa 5:12; Amos 6:5
In prison	Acts 16:25

SINLESSNESS *(See also Perfection)*

Of Christ	Luke 1:35; John 8:46; 2 Cor 5:21
Beyond human ability	Rom 3:23; 1 John 1:8

SINNER *(See also Evil, Sin, Unbeliever)*

Class of all men	Rom 3:23
Punishment of	Prov 11:31; Rom 6:23

Jesus' relationship to:

Friend of	Luke 7:34
Came to invite	Luke 5:32
Welcomes	Luke 15:1–2
Savior	Acts 2:36–38

SLANDER *(See also Backbiting, Gossip, Tongue)*

Do not listen to	1 Sam 24:9
Bad effects of	Prov 16:28; 18:8; 19:9; 26:20
Enduring for Christ's sake	Matt 5:11
Of evil heart	Luke 6:45
Returning good for	1 Cor 4:13
Christians should not	2 Cor 12:20; Eph 4:29–31

SLEEP *(See also Insomnia, Rest)*

Supernaturally caused	Gen 2:21; 1 Sam 26:12

Visions in	Gen 28:10; 1 Sam 3:2–18; Dan 8:18
Meaning physical death	John 11:11–14
Of the lazy	Prov 6:9–10; 24:33
Of disciples	Matt 26:40–43
Figuratively, spiritual state of the unsaved	Eph 5:14

SMOKING (See Health)

SOCIAL REFORM (See also Justice, Poverty, Society)

How to help the poor	Prov 19:17; 22:2, 9; Luke 3:11
How to treat the poor	Prov 14:20–21, 31; 19:7

SOCIETY (See also Justice, Liberality, Witnessing)
Christian's responsibility:

To be salt	Matt 5:13
To be light	Matt 5:14; Gal 6:10
To obey those in authority	Rom 13:1
To pay taxes	Rom 13:6–7
To witness	1 Pet 2:9–10
To act justly and love mercy	Isa 1:16–17; Mic 6:8

SODOM (See also Gomorrah)

Its sin and destruction	Gen 13:13; 18:20–19:29
Lot escaped	Gen 19:1–26
An example of God's judgment	Matt 10:15; Luke 17:29; Rev 11:8

SOLDIER (See also Battle, War)

Of Israel	Num 1:2
Mocked Jesus	Matt 27:27–31

196

Crucified Jesus   *Matt 27:27, 31–37; John 19:23–24*
Guarding tomb   *Matt 27:65; 28:4, 11–15*

SOLOMON

Birth and parents of   *2 Sam 5:14*
Rise to kingship   *1 Kings 1:28*
Wisdom of   *1 Kings 4:29–31*
Folly of   *1 Kings 11:1–8*
Built temple   *1 Kings 6:1*

SON *(See also Adoption, Daughter, Family)*

Of Man   *Matt 12:40; 24:37–44; Luke 19:10*
Of God—Christ   *Mark 1:1; Luke 1:35; John 1:34*
Of God—believer   *Gal 3:26*

SONG *(See also Hymn, Music, Singing)*

Of praise   *2 Chron 5:18; Acts 16:25*
New   *Ps 33:3*
At Passover   *Matt 26:30*
Spiritual   *Eph 5:19; Col 3:16*

SORROW *(See also Grief, Mourning, Tear)*

God sees   *Gen 21:17–20; Exod 3:7–10*
Of Jacob for Joseph   *Gen 37:34–35*
Shall go away   *Isa 35:10*
Of Jesus   *Isa 53:11; Matt 26:37–44*
Of the lost   *Matt 8:12; 13:42, 50; 22:13*
Because of sin   *2 Cor 7:10–11*
None in heaven   *Rev 21:4*

SOUL *(See also Heart, Mind, Person)*

Man became a living	*Gen 2:7*
At death	*Gen 35:18*
Loving God with all of	*Matt 22:37*
To serve with	*Josh 22:5*
Impatience of	*Num 21:4*
Redemption of	*Lev 17:11*
Worth of	*Matt 16:26*

SOVEREIGNTY *(See also Authority, Ruler)*

Of God:

His ownership	*Ps 24:1; 50:10*
His reign	*Exod 15:18; Josh 2:11; Rom 14:11*
His greatness	*Exod 18:11; Deut 4:39; 10:14*
Over life	*1 Sam 2:6; Dan 5:23; Col 1:17*
Over man's ways	*1 Sam 2:7–8; Job 34:24; John 19:11*
Over salvation	*John 10:29; James 4:12*

SPEECH *(See also Conversation, Tongue, Voice)*

With grace	*Col 4:6*
Moses claimed to be slow of	*Exod 4:10*
Paul's was not eloquent	*1 Cor 1:17*
Of false teachers	*Rom 16:18*

SPIRIT *(See also Fruit of the Spirit, Holy Spirit)*

Of evil	*1 Sam 16:16; 18:10; Hos 4:12*
Holy	*Ps 51:11; Isa 63:10; Matt 12:32*
Control of one's	*Prov 16:32; 25:28*
Body apart from	*James 2:26*
Does not die with body	*Matt 27:50; Acts 7:59*

SPIRITUALISM *(See also Occult, Spirit, Witchcraft)*

Condemned	*Lev 19:26; Deut 18:9–14; Isa 47:13*
Of mediums	*Deut 18:11; 1 Sam 28:8; 2 Kings 21:6*
As divination	*1 Sam 15:23; Ezek 21:21*

SPIRITUALITY *(See also Discipleship, Holy Spirit, Sanctification)*

True:

Because of Holy Spirit	*Rom 8:4*
Devotion to God	*Deut 6:5; 1 Kings 8:23*
Trust	*Isa 26:3; Rom 8:6*
Perception	*Mark 2:8; Acts 17:16; Gal 6:1*
Discernment	*John 16:13; 1 Cor 2:14–15*
Holiness	*2 Cor 7:1; Col 2:5*

SPRING *(See also Thirst, Water)*

Source of water for earth	*Ps 104:10*
Jesus asked for drink from	*John 4:7*
Cannot produce two kinds of water	*James 3:11*
Without water likened to deceiver	*2 Pet 2:17*
Which gives eternal life	*John 4:13–14*

SPRINKLING *(See also Sacrifice)*

Of blood:

For tabernacle and people	*Lev 8:15, 19*
For leper	*Lev 14:7*
To cleanse flesh	*Heb 9:13*
Of Christ, figuratively	*1 Pet 1:2*

Of water:

For Levites	*Num 8:7*

| For Israel | Ezek 36:25 |
| For tabernacle and people | Heb 9:19–22 |

STAR (See also Astrology, Astronomy, Sun)

Created by God	Gen 1:16; Ps 8:3
Worshiped	Jer 8:2
Of Bethlehem	Matt 2:2

STATE (See also Government, Nation, Society)

God over Israel	Exod 19:5–6
Has its own rights	Luke 20:25
Exists by God's grace	John 19:11
Christians are to support	Rom 13:1–7; 1 Tim 2:2

STEADFASTNESS (See also Faithfulness, Long-suffering, Patience)

Of God	Num 23:19; James 1:17
In affliction	Ps 44:17–19; 1 Thess 3:3
In the early church	Acts 2:42
In the faith	1 Cor 16:13
Commanded	Phil 4:1; 2 Thess 2:15; James 1:6–8
In confidence	Heb 3:6, 14

STEALING (See Deceit, Dishonesty, Robbery)

Condemned	Exod 20:15; Deut 5:19; Matt 19:18
Repayment for	Exod 22:1–15; Lev 6:4–5
Causes shame	Jer 2:26
Work instead of	Eph 4:28

STEPHEN *(See also Martyrdom)*

Chosen as deacon	*Acts 6:5*
Arrested	*Acts 6:8–15*
His sermon	*Acts 7:1–53*
Was stoned to death	*Acts 7:54–60*

STERILITY *(See also Barrenness)*

Viewed as a reproach	*Gen 30:22–23*
Healed by God	*Gen 17:15–21; 25:21; 1 Sam 1:6–20*

STONE *(See also Foundation)*
Figurative:

Of offense	*Isa 8:14; Rom 9:33; 1 Pet 2:8*
Of hard heart	*Ezek 36:26*
Of Christ	*Matt 21:42; Acts 4:11; 1 Pet 2:4*

STONING

As capital punishment	*Exod 19:13; Heb 11:37*
Of Sabbath breaker	*Num 15:36*
Required witnesses	*Deut 13:9*
Of Achan	*Josh 7:25*
Of Naboth	*1 Kings 21:13*
Of Stephen	*Acts 7:59*
Of Paul	*Acts 14:19; 2 Cor 11:25*

STRENGTH *(See also Power, Weakness)*

Of the Lord	*Exod 13:3, 14, 16*
Of man	*Exod 15:2; Ps 28:7; 46:1*
Given to the weak by God	*Isa 40:29*
Loving God with	*Mark 12:30*

Supplied by God   *1 Pet 4:11*

STRESS *(See also Anxiety, Care, Worry)*
Exhibited by Paul   *1 Cor 2:3; 2 Cor 7:5*
Eased by Titus and the Corinthians   *2 Cor 7:6–7*
Exhibited by Christ   *Luke 22:42–44*

STRIFE *(See also Arguing, Quarrel)*
Avoided   *Prov 15:18*
Spread by the perverse   *Prov 16:28*
Is difficult to stop   *Prov 17:14*
Brought by fools   *Prov 18:6*
Not to be among Christians   *Rom 13:13; 1 Cor 3:3*
Leads to confusion and evil   *James 3:16*

STUBBORNNESS *(See also Pride, Rebellion)*
Of Pharaoh   *Exod 4:21; 7:3, 13, 22*
In believing   *2 Chron 36:15–16*
In not listening   *Prov 1:24*
In resisting the Holy Spirit   *Acts 7:51*
In not repenting   *Rom 2:5*

STUMBLING *(See also Stone)*
Caused by sin   *Ezek 7:19; Rom 11:9–11*
Block (stone):
The blind   *Lev 19:14*
Figurative:
As an offense   *Rom 9:32–33*
Not causing a brother's   *Rom 14:13; 1 Cor 8:9*

SUBMISSION *(See also Humility, Love, Servant)*

To righteousness of God	*Rom 10:3*
To one another	*Eph 5:21*
Of wife to husband	*Eph 5:22; Col 3:18*
To human institution	*1 Pet 2:13*
To elders	*1 Pet 5:5*
To leaders	*Heb 13:7*
To God	*James 4:7*

SUBSTITUTION *(See also Atonement)*

Of offering for offerer	*Lev 1:4; 16:21–22*
Of Jesus for Barabbas	*Matt 27:20; Mark 15:11*
Dying in place of a friend	*John 15:13*
Christ's suffering in place of man's	*1 Pet 2:21*

SUCCESS *(See also Blessing, Reward)*

Obtained by:

Requesting from God	*Gen 24:12*
Keeping God's Word	*Josh 1:8*

As prosperity:

From God	*Gen 33:11; Ps 127:1; 128:1–2*
Danger of	*Deut 8:10–18; 2 Chron 12:1; 26:16*

SUFFERING *(See also Adversity, Affliction, Pain)*

Because of sin	*Gen 3:15–19; Hos 8:7; Gal 6:8*
As a chastisement	*Judg 2:22–3:6; Prov 3:12*
As a test	*Ps 66:10; James 1:3, 12; 1 Pet 1:7*
God's presence in	*Ps 73:21–26*
In God's control	*Isa 45:7; Amos 3:6; Acts 2:23*
Sharing in Christ's	*Mark 10:39; Rom 8:17*

Of Christ   *Heb 12:2; 1 Pet 1:10–12; 2:24*

SUICIDE
Of Saul   *1 Sam 31:4*
Of Saul's armor bearer   *1 Sam 31:5*
Of Judas   *Matt 27:5*
Saving jailer from   *Acts 16:27–28*
Jews question Jesus' intent   *John 8:22*

SUN
Made by God   *Gen 1:16*
Stood still   *Josh 10:13*
Protection from   *Ps 121:6*
Figuratively:
Of the righteous   *Matt 13:43*
Of Christ's glory   *Matt 17:2*

SUNDAY *(See Lord's Day)*

SUPERSTITION *(See also Idolatry)*
Instances of:
Burning incense to restore prosperity   *Jer 44:17–19*
Bringing the ark to assure victory   *1 Sam 4:3–10*
Casting lots to determine who caused evil   *Jon 1:7–8*
Jews used in accusing Paul   *Acts 25:19*

SUPPER *(See also Last Supper)*
Christ and disciples   *Matt 26:17–30*
Communion   *1 Cor 11:20–32*
For believers in heaven   *Rev 19:9*

For those who can't reciprocate   *Luke 14:12–14*
In honor of Jesus   *John 12:2*

SWEARING *(See also Blasphemy, Oath)*

To not deal falsely   *Gen 21:23–24*
By the name of the Lord   *Isa 48:1*
As cursing   *Mark 14:71*
Jesus preached against   *Matt 5:34–37*
By God in his covenant with Abraham   *Heb 6:13*

SWORD *(See also Armor, Judgment, War)*

Flaming   *Gen 3:24*
Beat into plowshares   *Mic 4:3*
Christ warns about use of   *Matt 25:51–52*
James killed by   *Acts 12:2*
Figuratively:
Two-edged   *Rev 1:16*
Of the word of God   *Heb 4:12*
Of the Spirit   *Eph 6:17*

SYMBOL *(See also Cross, Communion, Type)*

Rainbow   *Gen 9:13–15*
Oil   *Ps 45:7*
Water   *Eph 5:26*
Dove   *Matt 3:16*
Smitten rock   *1 Cor 10:4*
Baptism   *Rom 6:3–4*
Lord's Supper   *1 Cor 11:23–26*

SYMPATHY *(See also Compassion, Pity)*

For prisoners	*Heb 13:3*
For fatherless and widows	*James 1:27*
For one another	*1 Pet 3:8*
For the multitudes	*Matt 15:32*
Of God	*Jon 4:2*
Such as Christ showed	*Phil 2:2–5*

SYNAGOGUE *(See also Church, Temple)*

Hypocritical giving in	*Matt 6:2*
Pharisees love chief seats in	*Matt 23:6*
Christ read and interpreted Scripture in	*Luke 4:16–27*
Persecuted in	*Mark 13:9*

T

TABERNACLE *(See also Ark of the Covenant)*

Instruction for building	*Exod 26*
Completed	*Exod 39:32*
Glory of the Lord filled	*Exod 40:34*
True one set up by the Lord	*Heb 8:2*
Figuratively:	
Of the body	*2 Pet 1:13–14*
Of God's presence with man	*Rev 21:3*

TABLE *(See also Lord's Supper)*

For the shewbread	*Exod 25:30*
Of the Lord	*1 Cor 10:21*
Christ betrayed at	*Luke 22:21*

To serve, indicating charitable work   *Acts 6:2*
Of stone   *Exod 24:12*

TACT *(See Discretion, Mouth, Prudence)*

TALENT *(See also Creativity, Gift)*
Not to neglect   *1 Tim 4:14*
Parable on use of   *Matt 25:14–30*
Use of according to ability   *Rom 12:6*
To use for one another   *1 Pet 4:10*

TARSHISH
Where Jonah headed in disobedience   *Jon 1:3*
Prophecies concerning   *Ps 48:7; 72:10; Isa 2:16; 60:9*

TARSUS
Apostle Paul's hometown   *Acts 9:11*

TAXES *(See also Publican)*
Collectors of   *Matt 5:46*
Of Caesar Augustus   *Luke 2:1*
Jesus paid   *Matt 17:24*
Jesus ate with collectors of   *Mark 2:16*
Commanded to pay   *Rom 13:6–7*
To Caesar   *Matt 22:17–21*

TEACHER *(See also Instruction, Learning, Wisdom)*
In early church   *Acts 13:1*
Gift to the church   *Eph 4:11*
Warning against false   *2 Pet 2:1*

Christ as   *Mark 1:21–22; Luke 24:;27; John 7:14*
Holy Spirit as   *John 14:26*

TEACHING *(See also Doctrine, Law)*

Of Christ   *Matt 5:1–12*
For meditation   *Ps 119:15–16*
Christ questioned about his   *John 18:19*
Scripture profitable for   *2 Tim 3:16*
People astonished at   *Matt 7:28*
Disciples how to pray   *Luke 11:1*

TEAR *(See also Sorrow, Weeping)*

Poured out to God   *Job 16:20*
Washed Christ's feet with   *Luke 7:38*
Of Christ   *Heb 5:7*
God shall wipe away   *Rev 7:17*
Absence of in heaven   *Rev 21:4*

TEMPERANCE *(See Abstinence from alcohol, Drunkenness, Liberty)*

TEMPLE *(See also Synagogue)*

House of the Lord   *1 Kings 6:1–2*
God's glory in   *Isa 6:1*
Herod's   *John 2:20*
Early Christians met in   *Acts 2:46*
Jesus drove money makers out of   *Luke 19:45*
Figurative:
Of Christ's body   *John 2:19–22*
Of Christian's body   *1 Cor 3:16–17*

TEMPTATION *(See also Trial)*

By Satan in garden	*Gen 3:1–5*
Eve yielded to	*Gen 3:6*
Prayer to avoid	*Matt 6:13*
Of Christ by Satan	*Luke 4:1–13*
Common to all	*1 Cor 10:13*
Reward for enduring	*James 1:12*
Is not from God	*James 1:13–14*

TEN COMMANDMENTS *(See also Commandment, Law, Moses)*

Given by God	*Exod 20:1–17*
Referred to by Christ	*Matt 5:21, 27, 31, 33, 38, 43*
Bring knowledge of sin	*Rom 7:7*
Summed up	*Rom 13:9*

TENDERNESS *(See also Gentleness, Kindness)*

Shown to one another	*Eph 4:32*
Of Christ in Paul's life	*2 Cor 10:1*
Characteristic of God	*James 5:11*

TENT *(See also Tabernacle)*

Of meeting	*Num 2:17*
Ark of Covenant in	*1 Chron 16:1*
Made by Paul, Priscilla, and Aquila	*Acts 18:2–3*
Figurative:	
Of the heavens	*Isa 40:22*
Of growth of Israel	*Isa 54:2*

209

TESTAMENT *(See also Covenant, Promise)*

Symbols of the New	*Matt 26:28; Luke 22:20*
Ministers of the New	*2 Cor 3:6*
Reading of the Old	*2 Cor 3:14*
Christ mediator of a New	*Heb 9:15*

TESTIMONY *(See also Covenant, Law, Witnessing)*

Placed in the ark	*Exod 25:16*
Of God's majesty to others	*Ps 145:11–12*
Of the Lord	*Ps 19:7*
Believed by others	*2 Thess 1:10*
Not to be ashamed of giving	*2 Tim 1:8*

THADDEUS *(See also Judas)*

Chosen as apostle	*Matt 10:3*

THANKFULNESS *(See also Gratitude, Ingratitude, Thanksgiving)*

God's will for believers	*Col 4:12; 1 Thess 5:18*
In Christ's name	*Eph 5:20*

Expressed for:

Wisdom	*Dan 2:23*
Answered prayer	*John 11:41*
Salvation	*2 Cor 9:15*
Food	*John 6:11, 23*

THANKSGIVING *(See also Praise, Thankfulness, Worship)*

Offered to God	*Ps 69:30; 100:4; 147:7*
To accompany prayer	*Phil 4:6*

Response of believer   *Col 2:7*

THEOPHILUS
To whom Luke's gospel is addressed   *Luke 1:3*

THESSALONICA
Paul's journey there   *Acts 17:1*

THIEF *(See also Robbery, Stealing)*
Crucified with Christ   *Matt 27:38, 44; Mark 15:27*
The Day of the Lord will come as a   *1 Thess 5:2*
Behavior condemned   *Exod 20:15*

THIRST *(See also Water)*
Satisfied   *Rev 7:16*
Figurative of:
Salvation   *Isa 55:1; John 7:37; Eph 4:28*
Desire to know God   *Ps 42:1; 63:1*
Longing for righteousness   *Matt 5:6*

THOMAS *(See also Apostle)*
Disciple of Jesus   *Matt 10:3*
Willing to die with Jesus   *John 11:16*
Resurrection appearances to   *John 20:19–29*
Present in upper room   *Acts 1:13*

THRONE *(See also King)*
Men's, established through righteousness   *Prov 16:12*
David's promised to Jesus Christ   *Luke 1:30–32*
Christ's eternal   *Luke 1:32–33*

211

| Christ now rules form | *Eph 1:20–23; Heb 1:3* |
| Christ will judge from | *Matt 25:31–32* |

TIME *(See also Season)*

Right, to respond to the gospel	*Mark 1:15*
Should be used carefully	*Eph 5:16*
Christ born at the right	*Gal 4:4*
Of Christ's return unknown	*Matt 24:36*
Appropriate, for different events	*Eccles 3:1–8*

TIMOTHY

Faith from childhood	*2 Tim 1:5*
Became Paul"s assistant	*Acts 16:1–3*
Ordained by elders	*1 Tim 4:14*
Loyal worker	*Phil 2:22*
Loved by Paul	*1 Tim 1:18*
Imitator of Paul	*1 Cor 4:17*
Prone to sickness	*1 Tim 5:23*

TITHE *(See also Offering)*

Given by Abraham to Melchizedek	*Heb 7:1–2, 6*
Possession of the Lord	*Lev 27:30–33*
Provision for Levites	*Num 18:21–24*
Promise regarding	*Mal 3:10–12*
Legalistic practice of Pharisees condemned	*Luke 11:42;*
	18:9–14

TITUS

| Greek coworker with Paul | *Gal 2:3; 2 Cor 7:6* |
| Paul's letter to | *Titus 1:1* |

TOLERANCE *(See also Intolerance, Patience)*

Religious	*Luke 9:49–50*
With a weaker brother	*Rom 14:1–18*
Inappropriate when treating sin	*Mark 9:43–48*

TONGUE *(See also Conversation, Mouth, Speech)*

Powerful instrument for good or evil	*James 3:5–11*
To be guarded carefully	*Ps 39:1; Prov 21:23*

Proper use of:

To proclaim God's righteousness	*Ps 35:28*
To speak on behalf of justice	*Ps 37:30*
To sing	*Ps 119:172; 126:2*
To confess Christ	*Phil 2:11*

TONGUES, GIFT OF *(See also Baptism)*

Experienced at Pentecost	*Acts 2:1–11*
Gift of the Holy Spirit	*1 Cor 12:10–11*
Interpreter required	*1 Cor 14:27–28*

TORMENT *(See also Suffering)*

Eternal	*Rev 14:9–11, 20:10*
Physical	*Matt 8:6*
Experienced by faithful	*Heb 11:35–39*

TRADITION *(See also Law, Teaching)*

Reject worldly	*Col 2:8*

Christian, described:

Fundamental truths	*1 Cor 15:3*
Passed on by apostles	*2 Thess 3:6–7; 2 Thess 2:15*
Based on eyewitness reports	*2 Pet 1:16*

Originating with Christ   *1 Cor 11:1, 23–26*

TREACHERY *(See also Deceit, Dishonesty)*
Revealed in:
Judas   *Matt 26:47–50; Mark 14:43–46*
David   *2 Sam 11:14–15*
Absalom   *2 Sam 13:23–29*
Haman   *Esther 3:5–11*

TREASON *(See also Patriotism)*
Examples of:
Rahab against Jericho   *Josh 2:1–21*
Absalom against David   *2 Sam 15:1–14*
Athaliah against Judah   *2 Kings 11*

TREASURE *(See also Riches)*
Tabernacle used for   *Num 31:54; Josh 6:19–24*
Solomon's temple used for   *1 Kings 7:51*
Figurative of:
New life in Jesus Christ   *2 Cor 4:6–7*
Wisdom   *Prov 2:4*
Spiritual understanding   *Matt 13:52; Col 2:2–3*

TREE *(See also Branch)*
Figurative of:
Righteous   *Ps 1:1–3*
Works of righteous   *Prov 11:30*
Wisdom   *Prov 3:18*
Eternal life   *Gen 3:22, 24; Rev 22:14*

TRIAL *(See also Adversity, Affliction, Discipline)*

Test and prove faith	*Gen 22:1–14*
Purify faith	*1 Pet 1:6–9*
Suffered as Christian	*1 Pet 4:12–16*
Develops perseverance	*James 1:3*
Sometimes severe	*2 Cor 1:8–11*

TRIBES OF ISRAEL

Named for 12 sons of Jacob	*Gen 49*

TRIBULATION *(See also Adversity, Suffering, Trouble)*

In the world	*John 16:33; Acts 14:22*
To increase in the end times	*Matt 24:21*
Results in patience	*Rom 5:3*
Known by God	*Rev 2:9*

TRINITY *(See also God, Holy Spirit, Jesus Christ)*

Revealed at Jesus' baptism	*Matt 3:16–17*
Jesus commanded to baptize in name of	*Matt 28:19*

Same work attributed to three members of:

Creation	*Gen 1:1; Ps 104:30; Col 1:16*
Salvation	*2 Thess 2:13–14; Titus 3:4–6; 1 Pet 1:2*

TROAS

Where Paul had vision	*Acts 16:8–9*

TROUBLE *(See also Adversity, Affliction, Temptation)*

As test of faith	*James 1:2–3; 1 Pet 1:7*
As judgment	*Ps 107:17*
As sign of God's love	*Heb 12:5–6*

God is faithful in	*Rom 8:35–39*
God comforts those in	*Matt 5:4*
Believers should be patient in	*1 Pet 2:20*

TRUMPET

Will be sounded at:

Christ's coming	*Matt 24:31; 1 Thess 4:16*
Judgment	*Rev 8:2, 13*

TRUST *(See also Belief, Confidence, Faith)*

With whole heart	*Prov 3:5*
In the Word of God	*Ps 119:42*
Not in man	*Ps 118:89; Jer 17:5*
Not in wealth	*Prov 11:28; Luke 12:19–20*

In the Lord:

Forever	*Isa 26:4*
For peace	*Isa 26:3*
For safety	*Prov 29:25*

TRUTH *(See also Honesty, Integrity, Truthfulness)*

Attribute of God	*Isa 65:16*
Spirit of	*John 15:26*
Christ is	*John 14:6*
Word of God is	*John 17:17*
Church is bulwark of	*1 Tim 3:15*
Believing the	*2 Thess 2:12*

TRUTHFULNESS *(See also Deceit, Honesty, Truth)*

In speech	*Prov 12:19*
In witness	*Prov 14:25*

Speaking to one another in   *Zech 8:16*
Christ became a servant to show   *Rom 15:8*

TYCHICUS
Companion of Paul   *Acts 20:4; 2 Tim 4:12; Titus 3:12*
Commended   *Eph 6:21; Col 4:7*

TYPE *(See also Symbol)*
Adam   *Rom 5:14*
Melchizedek   *Heb 7:1–17*
Paschal Lamb   *1 Cor 5:7*
Tabernacle   *Heb 8:5*
Bride   *Rev 2:12, 9; 22:17*

TYRANNY *(See also Government)*
Judged by God:
Poor avenged   *Isa 1:23–25*
Oppressor exiled   *Hos 5:10*
God spoke against   *Ezek 45:9*
God will abandon those guilty of   *Mic 3:1–4*

TYRE
Its wealth and fall   *Ezek 26:7–28:19*

U

UNBELIEF *(See also Belief, Unbeliever)*
In Word of God   *Ps 106:24; John 5:38*

In miracles   *Num 14:11–12; John 12:37*
A cry to overcome   *Mark 9:24*
Judgment against   *2 Thess 2:12; Jude 5*
Warning against   *John 3:36; Heb 3:12*

UNBELIEVER *(See also Belief, Disciple, Heathen)*
Mind and conscience are corrupt   *Titus 1:15*
Is condemned   *John 3:18*
Paul speaks about:
Lawsuits against   *1 Cor 6:6*
Reaction to speaking in tongues   *1 Cor 14:23*
Marriage to   *2 Cor 6:14*

UNCLEANNESS *(See also Cleanliness, Purity)*
Ceremonial   *Lev 13:3, 14, 25*
Caused by touching   *Lev 11:8; Acts 10:11–14*
Comes from within   *Matt 15:11, 18*
Is sin   *Eph 4:19*

UNDERSTANDING *(See also Knowledge, Wisdom)*
Man lacking   *Ps 14:1–4; Rom 3:11*
Blessing of   *Prov 3:13–15*
Asking for   *Ps 119:27*
Given by God to:
Bezalel   *Exod 31:1–3*
Solomon   *1 Kings 3:12*

UNFAITHFULNESS *(See also Backsliding, Idolatry, Loyalty)*
Judgment of   *Matt 3:10; 21:43*

Parables of	*Isa 5:1–7; Mark 12:1–9*
Examples of:	
By leaders	*Jer 6:13–15*
By Israel	*Hos 4:1*

UNITY *(See also Communion of Saints, Fellowship)*

Of believers:	
In Christ	*John 15:4–7; 1 Cor 3:23; Gal 2:20*
In Church	*Gal 3:28*
In mind and spirit	*1 Cor 1:10; Phil 1:27; 1 Pet 3:8*
Illustrated by:	
Body	*Rom 12:4–5; 1 Cor 10:17*
Husband and wife	*Eph 5:25–32*

UNPARDONABLE SIN *(See also Forgiveness)*

Blasphemy against Holy Spirit	*Matt 12:31–32; Mark 3:29*

UNSELFISHNESS *(See also Humility, Love)*

In living	*Matt 16:24–25; 1 Cor 10:24*
In true love	*1 Cor 13:4–5*
Examples of:	
Abraham	*Gen 13:8–9*
David	*1 Chron 21:17*
Paul	*1 Cor 9:12–22; 10:33*
Christ	*Mark 6:30–34; Rom 15:1–3*

UR

Land of Abraham's birth	*Gen 11:28; 15:7*

URIAH

The Hittite, husband of Bathsheba	*2 Sam 11:2-3*
Killed by David's order	*2 Sam 11:14-17*

UZZIAH

King of Judah	*2 Chron 26:1-23*
Instructed by Zechariah	*2 Chron 26:5*
Pride caused his downfall	*2 Chron 26:16-21*

V

VANITY *(See also Pride)*

Thoughts are	*Rom 1:21; Eph 4:17-19*
Results from the fall	*Rom 8:20*
Is the state of every man	*Ps 62:9; 39:5-6*
Days of man are	*Job 7:16; Eccles 1:2; 2:21*

VEIL

Of Tabernacle and Temple:

To conceal Holy of Holies	*Exod 40:3*
Described	*Exod 26:31-33*
Torn at Christ's death	*Matt 27:51*

Figurative of:

Spiritual blindness	*2 Cor 3:14-16*
The flesh of Christ	*Heb 10:20*

VENGEANCE *(See also Retaliation, Revenge)*

Forbidden to man	*Matt 5:38-39*
Belongs to God	*Deut 32:35; Prov 20:22*

On disobedient nations   *Mic 5:15*

VICTORY *(See also Battle, Joy, Overcoming)*
God assured   *Deut 20:4*
God gave to David   *2 Sam 8:6; 1 Chron 18:6*
Brought joy   *Ps 20:5*
Belongs to the Lord   *Prov 21:31*
Over death   *1 Cor 15:54*
Through faith   *1 John 5:4*

VINE *(See also Agriculture, Branch)*
Fruitfulness of   *Joel 2:22*
Unfruitfulness of   *Jer 8:13*
Figurative of:
Israel's unfaithfulness   *Ps 80:8–19*
Christ and believers   *John 15*
Judgment   *Ezek 15:6; Rev 14:18–19*

VIRGIN *(See also Celibacy, Chastity)*
Remaining as a   *1 Cor 7:25–26*
Figurative of:
Israel   *Jer 14:17*
Church   *2 Cor 11:2*
Believers   *Matt 25:1–9*
Birth:
Prophesied   *Isa 7:14*
Fulfilled   *Matt 1:23, 25*

VIRTUE *(See also Character, Goodness, Righteousness)*
Resulting from faith   *2 Pet 1:5*

Christians possess   *Rom 15:14; Gal 5:22*

VISION *(See also Dream, Eye, Revelation)*
Of true prophets   *Joel 2:28*
Of false prophets   *Jer 14:14; 23:16*
Examples of:
Jacob   *Gen 46:2*
Prophets   *Isa 6; Dan 7*
The Apostle John   *Rev 1:9–20*

VOCATION *(See also Calling, Career, Work)*
Living worthy of   *Eph 4:1*

VOICE *(See also Singing, Speech)*
Of God:
Powerful   *Job 40:9; Ps 68:33*
Whisper   *1 Kings 19:12*
From heaven   *Matt 3:17; 17:5; Acts 9:4–6*

VOW *(See also Oath, Promise)*
To be taken with care   *Prov 20:25*
Made to God:
Example of   *Gen 28:20*
Should be fulfilled   *Num 30:2; Deut 23:21*

W

WAITING *(See also Impatience, Patience)*
For promise of God   *Acts 1:4*

For coming of Christ	1 Cor 1:7; 1 Thess 1:10
For fulfillment of God's words	Hab 2:3
For guidance and teaching	Ps 25:5

Upon God:

| Encouraged | Ps 27:14 |
| Blessing of | Isa 40:31 |

WALK (See also Conversation, Way)

| With God | Gen 5:24; 6:9 |

Figurative:

Before God	Gen 17:1; Ps 116:9
In light	1 John 1:7
In love	Eph 5:2
In the spirit	Gal 5:16
In new life	Rom 6:4
In truth	2 John 4; 3 John 3

WALL (See also Protection)

Of Cities:

| Destruction caused grief | Deut 28:52; Neh 1:3; 1 Kings 20:30 |

Figurative of:

Salvation	Isa 26:1; 60:18
Separation	Eph 2:13–14
Hypocrites	Acts 23:3

WAR (See also Armor, Army, Battle)

Originates in lust of men	James 4:1–2
Victory given by God	Num 21:3
As a judgment of God	2 Kings 15:37
To cease	Isa 2:4

Horrors of   *Ps 79:1–4*
Figurative of Christian life   *2 Cor 10:3; Eph 6:12*

WASHING *(See also Bathing, Cleansing, Purification)*
Ceremonial   *Exod 29:4*
Of feet   *Luke 7:44; John 13:5*
Of hands   *Ps 26:6; Matt 27:24*
Figurative of sins:
By God   *Isa 1:18; Eph 5:26*
Asking for   *Ps 51:7*
By blood of Christ   *1 John 1:7*

WATCHFULNESS *(See also Waiting)*
Against sin   *Matt 26:41*
For Second Coming   *Matt 25:13; 1 Thess 5:6; Rev 16:15*
Characterized by:
Prayer   *Eph 6:18*
Steadfastness   *1 Cor 16:13*

WATER *(See also Life, Purity, Thirst)*
Miracles involving   *Exod 14:21; John 2:9*
Figurative:
Of affliction   *Ps 42:7; Isa 30:20*
Of life   *Rev 7:17; John 4:10; 7:37–38*
Of Holy Spirit   *John 7:38–39; Isa 44:3*

WAVE OFFERING *(See also Offering)*
Given to Priests   *Exod 29:26–28; Lev 7:31, 34*
To be eaten in a holy place   *Lev 10:14*

Offered for:
  Consecration of priests   *Lev 8:29*
  Jealousy   *Num 5:25*
  Leper's trespass   *Lev 14:1, 12*

WAY *(See also Road, Walk)*
  To life   *Isa 26:7; Matt 7:14*
  That is perfect   *Ps 18:30; Dan 4:37*
  Above man's   *Isa 55:9; Rom 11:33*
  Guidance for   *Prov 3:6; Isa 42:16*
  Descriptive of early Christians   *Acts 19:19*
Figurative of:
  Christ   *John 14:6; Heb 10:20*
  The wicked   *Ps 35:6; Prov 4:19; 15:9*

WEAKNESS *(See also Strength)*
  Of God stronger than men   *1 Cor 1:25*
Of Men:
  Caused by sin   *Josh 7:12; Mark 9:18*
  Cared for by God   *Ps 116:6*
  Leads to dependency on God   *2 Cor 3:5*
  Christ sympathetic with   *Heb 4:15*

WEALTH *(See Money, Riches)*

WEAPON *(See also Armor, Battle)*
  Wisdom better than   *Eccles 9:18*
  Shall be destroyed   *Ezek 39:9–10*
Figurative of:
  Nations   *Jer 51:20*

Righteousness   *2 Cor 10:4*
Divine power   *2 Cor 6:7*
God's wrath   *Isa 13:5; Jer 50:25*

WEEPING *(See also Grief, Sorrow, Tear)*
In grief   *Gen 21:16; 1 Sam 1:6–8; Acts 20:37*
Caused by sin   *Deut 1:45; Jer 3:21*
In hell   *Matt 8:12; 24:51*
Leads to joy   *Ps 30:5; Luke 6:21*
At tomb of Christ   *John 20:15*

WEIGHTS AND MEASURES
Fairness in   *Lev 19:35, 36; Prov 11:1*

WELFARE *(See also Charity, Poor People, Society)*
Abundant in following wisdom   *Prov 3:1–2*
God's concern for the poor and oppressed   *Prov 14:31;*
                                              Isa 58:6–11

Of God's people:
God delights in   *Ps 35:27*
Jeremiah accused of not caring for   *Jer 38:4*

WHEAT *(See also Agriculture)*
In offerings   *Num 18:12; 1 Chron 21:23*
Parable of   *Matt 13:25; Luke 16:7*

WHEEL
Used to thresh grain   *Isa 28:27*
Of potter   *Jer 18:3*
Symbolic   *Ezek 1:15–21; 3:13; 10:9–19; 11:22*

Figurative of life ending   *Eccles 12:6*

WHITE *(See also Color)*
Descriptive of:

Clothing   *Matt 17:2; Rev 3:5; 4:4*

Angels   *Matt 28:3; Acts 1:10*

Harvest   *John 4:35*

Symbolic of:

Cleansing from sin   *Isa 1:18; Dan 12:10*

Purity   *Rev 2:17; 6:2*

WICKEDNESS *(See also Abomination, Evil, Sin)*

Suppresses truth   *Rom 1:18*

Detested   *Prov 8:7*

Brings wrath of God   *Gen 6:5–7; Isa 9:18–19*

Becomes object of reproach   *Ezek 16:56–58*

WIDOW *(See also Orphan)*

Allowed to glean fields   *Deut 24:19; Ruth 2:2*

Oppression of forbidden   *Exod 22:22; Zech 7:10*

May remarry   *1 Cor 7:39; 1 Tim 5:11–15*

Levitical laws concerning   *Deut 24:19; Ruth 3:10–13*

Provision for:

By God   *Deut 10:18; Prov 15:25*

By church   *Acts 6:1–3; 1 Tim 5:9*

By relatives   *1 Tim 5:16*

WIFE *(See also Husband, Marriage)*

Becomes one with husband   *Gen 2:24; Matt 19:5–6*

Blessing from God   *Prov 12:4; 18:22*

Duties of	*Prov 31:27; Titus 2:4–5*
Should:	
Be modest	*1 Tim 2:9*
Do good	*1 Tim 2:10; 5:10*
Have a quiet spirit	*1 Pet 3:4–5*

WILDERNESS

Place of testing	*Mark 1:12; Heb 3:8*
Place of refuge	*1 Sam 26:3; Luke 4:42; Rev 12:6*
Voice in	*Isa 40:3; Matt 3:3*
Made fruitful	*Isa 41:18*

WILL, LAST TESTAMENT

Of Abraham	*Gen 25:5–6*
Of Jacob	*Gen 48:3–49:28*
Of David	*2 Kings 2:1–9*
Not to be annulled	*Gal 3:15*
Enforced after death	*Heb 9:16–17*

WILL OF GOD *(See also Guidance, Predestination)*

Christ's resignation to	*Matt 26:39; John 6:38–39*
Asking for	*Matt 6:10*
Directing early missions	*Acts 18:21; Rom 15:30–32*
That Christians abstain from immorality	*1 Thess 4:3*

WILL OF MAN *(See also Self-will)*

Free to choose good or evil	*Josh 24:15; Deut 30:19*
In bondage to sin	*Prov 5:22; Rom 6:16*
Set free by Christ	*2 Tim 2:26*
To be inclined towards God	*Deut 5:29; Isa 1:19*

WIND *(See also Spirit, Holy Spirit)*

Providential	*Gen 8:1*
Of pestilence	*Jer 4:11*

Miracles with:

Bringing locusts	*Exod 10:13, 19*
Calmed by Christ	*Matt 8:26–27; 14:32*

Figurative of:

Life of men	*Job 7:7*
Work of Spirit	*Ezek 37:9; John 3:8*
False doctrine	*James 1:6*

WINE *(See also Drinking, Drunkenness, Vine)*

For enjoyment	*Ps 104:15*
Water turned into	*John 2:9*

In excess:

Forbidden	*Eph 5:18*
Leads to sorrow	*Prov 23:29–30*

Symbolic of:

Blood of Christ	*Matt 26:27–29*
Judgment of God	*Ps 60:3; Jer 13:12–14*

WISDOM *(See also Knowledge, Learning, Philosophy)*

Christ as believers'	*1 Cor 1:30; Col 2:3*
Value of	*Job 28:12–28; Prov 8:11; Eccles 7:19*
Given by God	*Eccles 2:26; James 1:5*
Prayers for	*2 Chron 1:10; Ps 90:12; Eph 1:17*
Characteristic of Christ	*Matt 13:54; Luke 2:40*
Personified	*Prov 8:1*

WITCHCRAFT (See also Astrology, Magic, Occult)

A sin	*Lev 19:31; 20:6; Gal 5:20*
Practitioners to be destroyed	*Exod 22:18; Mic 5:12*
Is vain	*Isa 8:19; 19:3–4*

Examples of:

Witch of Endor	*1 Sam 28:7*
Jezebel	*2 Kings 9:22*

WITNESS (See also Apostle, Evangelism, Witnessing)

Christian to be a	*Acts 1:8*
Two required	*Num 35:30; Matt 18:16*
Corrupted by money	*Matt 28:11–15; Acts 36:11–14*

Of Holy Spirit:

To Christ	*John 15:26; Acts 5:32; 1 John 5:8*
Given to believers	*Acts 15:8; Rom 8:16; 1 John 3:24*

WITNESSING (See also Evangelism, Witness)

Paul before King Agrippa	*Acts 26:22*
As a Christian	*1 Pet 3:15*

Examples of:

Andrew	*John 1:40–42*
Woman at the well	*John 4:28–30*
John the Baptist	*John 3:27, 31–36*

WOMAN (See also Man, Wives, Motherhood)

Creation of	*Gen 1:27; 2:21–23*
Devout	*1 Sam 1:15; Luke 1:25; Rom 16:1*
Believers, heirs with Christ	*Gal 3:26–29*

WORD OF GOD (See also Scripture)

Given by inspiration	1 Cor 2:12; 2 Tim 3:16; 2 Pet 1:21
Testifies to Jesus Christ	John 5:39; 20:30; Heb 1:1
Faithful and true	Rev 22:6
Eternal	Mark 13:31
To hear and understand	Matt 13:23
Obeying it brings blessing	Luke 11:28

Compared to:

A sword	Eph 6:17; Heb 4:12
Seed	Luke 8:11

WORK (See also Business, Career, Vocation)

Physical:

Forbidden on Sabbath	Exod 23:12; Deut 5:12–13
Be diligent in	Eccles 9:10; Col 3:23; 1 Thess 4:11

Religious:

Illustrated by parables	Matt 21:28; 25:21
Of the Lord	1 Cor 15:58
Of salvation	Eph 2:8–10; Phil 2:12–13
With God's help	Rom 8:26; 1 Cor 3:6–9; 2 Cor 6:1

WORKS (See also Faith)

Of evil	John 7:7; James 3:14–16; Jude 14–16
Judging of	Ps 62:12; Matt 16:27; 2 Cor 5:10

Good:

Not for salvation	Matt 7:22; Rom 3:20; Eph 2:8–9
Encouraged in Christians	Matt 5:16; Titus 2:7; 1 Pet 2:12
Belief in Christ	John 6:28–29

Of God:

Are good	Gen 1:10, 18, 21

Unsearchable and great   *Ps 40:5; 92:4; 136:4*

WORLD *(See also Creation, Earth)*
Creation of   *Gen 1:1; Job 26:7; Heb 11:3*
End of   *Isa 34:4; 2 Pet 3:10–11; Rev 21:1*
Will pass   *Ps 102:25–26; 1 Cor 7:31; 2 Cor 4:18*
As God's footstool   *Isa 66:1; Matt 5:35; Acts 7:49*
System, separation from commanded   *Rom 12:2;*
                                          Eph 5:11; 1 John 2:15

WORLDLINESS *(See also Bad Company, Sin, World)*
Imitation of the godless   *1 Sam 8:19–20; Eph 2:2*
Warnings against   *Matt 12:26; Col 3:2; Titus 2:12*
Effects of:
Unbelief   *Matt 13:22; Col 2:8; 2 Tim 4:10*
Delusion   *Matt 24:38–39*
Unprofitable   *Eccles 2:11; Matt 6:19; Luke 9:25*

WORRY *(See also Anxiety, Care, Stress)*
Lack of trust in God   *Matt 6:31–31, 34*
Chokes spiritual life   *Matt 13:22*
Forbidden   *Matt 6:25; Luke 21:34; Phil 4:6*
Cast upon Christ   *1 Pet 5:7*

WORSHIP *(See also Praise, Prayer, Thanksgiving)*
Of God, commanded   *Exod 20:3; Deut 5:7; Matt 4:10*
Of Christ   *John 9:38; Heb 1:6; Rev 5:8–9*
Attitude in   *Lev 10:3; Ps 5:7; John 4:24*
Universal   *Ps 22:27; Rom 14:11; Phil 2:9–10*
Places of   *Jer 26:2; Acts 1:13–14; Col 4:15*

WRATH (See also Anger, Punishment)

Of man, forbidden	Ps 37:8; Eph 4:26; James 1:19
Cup of	Jer 25:15; Rev 14:10
Of God:	
Against the disobedient	Rom 1:18; 2:8; Eph 5:6
Against unbelief	John 3:36

WRITING (See also Scribe)

On stone	Deut 27:3; Josh 8:32
On the heart	Prov 3:3; 7:3; Jer 31:33; Heb 8:10
On paper:	
The Law	Deut 31:9
Documents	1 Sam 10:25; 1 Chron 9:1

XERXES (See Ahasuerus)

YEARS (See also Day, Season)

Sabbatical	Exod 23:11; Lev 25:4
Jubilee	Lev 25:10, 28; 27:17; Num 36:4; Ezek 46:17
One thousand:	
Satan bound	Rev 20:2–4, 7
As a day to God	Ps 90:4; 2 Pet 3:8

YOKE *(See also Bondage, Discipline, Punishment)*

Of Christ	*Matt 11:29–30*

Figurative of:

Oppression of kings	*1 Kings 12:4–14*
Oppression of nations	*Jer 28:1–14*
Sin	*Lam 1:14*

YOUTH *(See also Adolescence, Children, Old Age)*

Not to be despised	*2 Tim 4:12*
Remember God in	*Eccles 12:1*
Sins of	*Ps 25:7; Jer 32:30*

Examples of calling in:

David	*1 Sam 17:33*
Jeremiah	*Jer 1:4–8*
Samuel	*1 Sam 3:10–4:1*

Z

ZACCHEUS

Wanted to see Jesus	*Luke 19:2*

ZACHARIAH, ZECHARIAH

King of Israel	*2 Kings 14:29*
Prophet	*Zech 1:1*

ZACHARIAS

Father of John the Baptist	*Luke 1:6*
Struck dumb by angel for doubting	*Luke 1:18, 22*

ZADOK
Priest who anointed Solomon   *1 Kings 1:39*

ZEAL
Of God   *2 Kings 19:31; Isa 26:11; 37:32*
Misguided   *Rom 10:2*
Religious:
Encouraged   *1 Thess 2:11–12*
For Law   *Acts 21:20*
Exemplified by:
Moses   *Exod 2:12, 11:8; 32:19–20*
Jesus   *John 2:17; Acts 10:38*
Paul   *Acts 32:3*

ZEBULUN
Coming of Messiah there prophesied
    and fulfilled   *Isa 9:1, 6–7; Matt 4:13*

ZEDEKIAH (MATTANIAH)
King of Judah   *2 Kings 24:17; 25:1–7*

ZEPHANIAH
Prophesied during reign of Josiah   *Zeph 1:1*

ZERUBBABEL
Prince of Judah   *Ezra 2:2*

ZION *(See also Jerusalem, Kingdom)*
Fortress captured by David   *2 Sam 5:6–9*
Dwelling place of God   *Isa 8:18*

Figurative of:

Israel as God's people   2 Kings 19:21
Kingdom of God   Ps 125:1
City of God   Heb 12:22
Heaven   Rev 14:1